EX·LIBRIS·SUNE·GREGERSEN

Infinitives and Gerunds in Recent English

Also by Juhani Rudanko

COMPLEMENTATION AND CASE GRAMMAR

PRAGMATIC APPROACHES TO SHAKESPEARE

PREPOSITIONS AND COMPLEMENT CLAUSES

DIACHRONIC STUDIES OF ENGLISH COMPLEMENTATION PATTERNS

CORPORA AND COMPLEMENTATION

COMPLEMENTS AND CONSTRUCTIONS

THE FORGING OF FREEDOM OF SPEECH

CHANGES IN COMLEMENTATION IN BRITISH AND AMERICAN ENGLISH

DISCOURSES OF FREEDOM OF SPEECH

LINKING FORM AND MEANING

Juhani Rudanko

Infinitives and Gerunds in Recent English

Studies on Non-Finite Complements with Data from Large Corpora

Juhani Rudanko
Department of English
University of Tampere
Tampere, Finland

ISBN 978-3-319-46312-4   ISBN 978-3-319-46313-1 (eBook)
DOI 10.1007/978-3-319-46313-1

Library of Congress Control Number: 2016950856

© The Editor(s) (if applicable) and The Author(s) 2017

This work is subject to copyright. All rights are solely and exclusively licensed by the Publisher, whether the whole or part of the material is concerned, specifically the rights of translation, reprinting, reuse of illustrations, recitation, broadcasting, reproduction on microfilms or in any other physical way, and transmission or information storage and retrieval, electronic adaptation, computer software, or by similar or dissimilar methodology now known or hereafter developed.

The use of general descriptive names, registered names, trademarks, service marks, etc. in this publication does not imply, even in the absence of a specific statement, that such names are exempt from the relevant protective laws and regulations and therefore free for general use. The publisher, the authors and the editors are safe to assume that the advice and information in this book are believed to be true and accurate at the date of publication. Neither the publisher nor the authors or the editors give a warranty, express or implied, with respect to the material contained herein or for any errors or omissions that may have been made.

Cover illustration: Cover pattern © Melisa Hasan

Printed on acid-free paper

This Palgrave Macmillan imprint is published by Springer Nature
The registered company is Springer International Publishing AG
The registered company address is: Gewerbestrasse 11, 6330 Cham, Switzerland

Acknowledgments

It is my pleasure to thank Palgrave Macmillan for including the present work in their Palgrave Pivot series.

The chapters in this volume were written in the summer and autumn of 2015, when I had the good fortune to have Maija Kyytsönen as a part-time research assistant at the University of Tampere. She helped me in essential ways in the analysis of the material and the checking of the manuscript, and I want to thank her for her assistance. Over the years I have also had the good fortune to attend international conferences in English linguistics and to talk to some of the people whose work is referred to in this book, and I have learned a great deal from them. I also want to thank my students at the University of Tampere. Before I retired from my post at the University of Tampere at the end of January 2016, I was able to teach annual seminars on complementation for several years, and many of the students in the seminars raised searching questions, helping me to think some more about complementation and about variation and change in this area of English grammar. The two anonymous referees for the publisher also deserve my thanks for their comments. Of course, none of those mentioned, directly or indirectly, is in any way responsible for the faults and shortcomings that remain in the present work—I am the only person responsible for those.

Tampere, July 2016   Juhani Rudanko

Contents

1 Introduction — 1

2 Non-Finite Complements of the Verb *Consent* in Current American and British English — 11

3 Non-Finite Complements of the Adjective *Subject* in Recent American English — 27

4 The Semantics of *to* Infinitives and *of*-*ing* Complements: A Case Study on the Adjective *Ashamed* — 41

5 Lexico-Grammatical Creativity in American Soap Operas: A Case Study of the Transitive *into*-*ing* Pattern — 57

6 Concluding Observations — 77

References — 83

Index — 87

LIST OF CORPORA

CASO	Corpus of American Soap Operas
CLMET	Corpus of Late Modern English Texts
COCA	Corpus of Contemporary American English
COHA	Corpus of Historical American English
GloWbE	Global Web-Based English Corpus

LIST OF TABLES

Table 2.1	[+Choice] and [−Choice] lower predicates in *to* infinitive and *to -ing* complements of *consent* in the American English segment of the GloWbE Corpus	21
Table 2.2	[+Choice] and [−Choice] lower predicates in *to* infinitive and *to -ing* complements of *consent* in the British English segment of the GloWbE Corpus	22
Table 3.1	Frequencies of *to* infinitive and *to -ing* complements of the adjective *subject* in the different decades of COHA	30
Table 3.2	*To* infinitive and *to -ing* complements of the adjective *subject* in the nineteenth and twentieth centuries	32
Table 3.3	The verb *want* followed by a comma or a period in COHA from the 1810s to the 1880s	37
Table 4.1	[+Choice] and [−Choice] interpretation of *to* infinitive and *of -ing* complements of *ashamed* in COHA in the 1940s and 1950s	46
Table 4.2	[+Choice] and [−Choice] interpretations of *to* infinitive and *of -ing* complements of *ashamed* in COCA from 2000 to 2009	48
Table 5.1	Creative uses of matrix verbs with the transitive *into -ing* pattern in the American Soap Opera Corpus	64
Table 5.2	Semantic classes of creatively used matrix verbs with the transitive *into -ing* pattern	71

CHAPTER 1

Introduction

Abstract The central objective of this book is to shed new light on selected control constructions involving *to* infinitives and different types of gerundial *-ing* clauses in recent English. This chapter outlines the key ideas that are useful in the study of control. Since the book deals with non-finite sentential complements, one key idea is the notion of an understood subject. Further, the notions of subject control and object control are presented. A basic assumption adopted for the study of control is Bolinger's Principle, according to which a difference in form can be expected also to involve a difference in meaning. The chapter also offers descriptions of the main patterns of control that are investigated in more detail in the subsequent chapters. Corpus data are a key source of evidence in the investigations, and the main corpora to be used are introduced in the chapter.

Keywords Complementation · Complement taking predicate · Subject control · Object control · Understood subject

This book investigates the properties of a selected set of complementation patterns in English. A suitable point of departure for this introductory chapter is provided by the following statement on the nature of complements in Huddleston and Pullum (2002, 219):

> The most important property of complements in clause structure is that they are licensed by an appropriate verb.

Huddleston and Pullum (2002, 219) go on to illustrate their point for instance with the contrast between *mention* (*mention a letter,* **mention to a letter*) and *allude* (**allude a letter, allude to a letter*). Their statement about verbs selecting complements needs of course to be broadened, for verbs are not the only type of head that licenses a complement. Adjectives and nouns may likewise license complements, as witness the adjective *afraid* (*afraid of saying too much* versus **afraid into saying too much*) and the noun *opportunity* (*an opportunity of making a statement* versus **an opportunity into making a statement*). However, Huddleston and Pullum's statement is valuable in bringing out the key feature inhering in complementation. This is that verbs, adjectives and nouns may, in their capacity as heads, syntactically subcategorize for a certain type of phrasal constituent or for certain types of phrasal constituents. The verbs, adjectives and nouns that subcategorize for one or more complement types may be termed complement-taking predicates (or CTPs, for short).

At the same time, the relation between a complement-taking predicate and its complement is not arbitrary. Noonan writes:

> Complementation is basically a matter of matching a particular complement type to a particular complement-taking predicate. The basis for this matching is the semantic relation between predicate and complement that is inherent in the meaning of the CTP, defining the relation of the predicate to the action or state described in the embedded predication, and the discourse function of the complement itself. Additional factors in this matching are the semantic possibilities inherent in the morphology and syntax of the complement type. The complement type... either contributes or fails to contribute certain sorts of information to the construction as whole and so is intrinsically better suited for certain kinds of CTPs and to certain discourse functions. In this way, different complement types can be used with the same CTP, exploiting their inherent meaning potential. The choice of complementizer may also affect the meaning potential of a complement. (Noonan 1985, 90–91)

The matching problem and the potential semantic contribution of the complement to the sentence as a whole are at the heart of the analyses of sentential complements presented in this book. A basic assumption made here is that different complement types have different meanings, and that even when selected by the same complement-taking predicate, the usages in question are seldom, if ever, synonymous. Another way of putting the point is what has sometimes been called Bolinger's Generalization or

Bolinger's Principle. This is that a "difference in syntactic form always spells a difference in meaning" (Bolinger 1968, 127). This generalization expresses a methodological principle, but it does not specify what the meaning difference between any two different constructions may be. In a sense it defines a research task for investigators. It is a central purpose of this book to take steps toward resolving this issue in the case of two central types of non-finite sentential complements in English. These are the *to* infinitive and gerundial constructions.

A great deal has been written on complementation, including sentential complements, since the Chomskyan revolution in linguistics in the 1950s and the 1960s, and insights in works such as Rosenbaum (1967),[1] with its emphasis on structural representations and the reasons for them, remain valuable in work on complementation and argument structure today. The present book eschews some elaborate projections found in some later work, of the type AgrO, but offers basic bracketings, where appropriate, for the constructions discussed.

An assumption widely made in the study of sentential complementation, and made in this book, concerns the postulation of understood or covert subjects. For instance, consider the sentences in (1), where the sentential complement of the matrix verb *try* in (1a) is a *to* infinitive and that of the matrix verb *resort* in (1b) is a prepositional gerund.

(1) a. Matt tried to use his fists.
     b. Matt resorted to using his fists.

The idea of understood subjects in such sentences as those in (1a–b) was accepted by major traditional grammarians, including Otto Jespersen. He writes:

> Very often a gerund stands alone without any subject, but as in other nexuses (nexus-substantives, infinitives, etc.) the connexion of a subject with the verbal idea is always implied. (Jespersen 1940, 140)

The postulation of understood subjects for the subordinate clauses in (1a–b) makes it possible to represent the argument structure properties of the lower verbs in sentences (1a–b), *use* in each case, in a straightforward fashion. The subject argument of the higher verb is represented by the overt NP *Matt* in both sentences. As for the lower verb, its subject is represented by the covert NP PRO, an "abstract pronominal element"

(Chomsky 1981, 6; see also Chomsky 1986, 114–131 and Davies and Dubinsky 2004, 84). The higher, overt subjects in (1a–b) are assigned semantic roles by the higher verbs, *try* and *resort*, respectively, and the lower subjects are assigned semantic roles by the lower verbs, *use* in each case. In the sentences in (1a–b) the semantic roles are the same for the higher and lower subjects in each sentence, for both subjects are Agents. However, it is easy to think of cases where they are not the same, as in (2a–b):

(2) a. Matt wanted to use his fists.
 b. Matt imagined using his fists.

In (2a) and (2b) the overt subjects of the higher verbs are assigned the semantic roles of Experiencer by the higher verbs, but the lower subjects are still Agents. Such discrepancies in semantic roles between higher and lower subjects are easy to conceptualize with the help of understood subjects. Understood subjects, once they are accepted, also provide a convenient way for accounting for the binding of anaphors, including reflexives, as for instance in *Having to perjure himself bothered Matt*, where a PRO subject of the infinitival clause binds the reflexive anaphor *himself*, with another PRO, controlled by the NP *Matt* in the higher clause, preceding *having*.

Accepting understood subjects in sentences of the type of (1a–b) and (2a–b), it is then possible to say that all four sentences display subject control, with the understood subject controlled by—interpreted as coreferential with—the higher subject in each case.

Chapters 2 through 4 of this book concern subject control constructions. In Chap. 2 the focus is on two types of subject control constructions selected by the verb *consent* in English. The two types are illustrated in the sentences in (3a–b), from the United States part of the Global Web-Based English Corpus, the GloWbE Corpus.

(3) a. …he consented to go on. (cs.smu.edu)
 b. I do not consent to giving up these rights at any time. (420magazine.com)

Given the assumption of understood subjects, the sentences in (3a–b), in their relevant parts, may be represented as in (3a′) and (3b′).

(3) a'. [[he]$_{NP}$ [consented]$_{Verb}$ [[PRO]$_{NP}$ [to]$_{Aux}$ [go on]$_{VP}$]$_{S2}$]$_{S1}$
   b'. [[I]$_{NP}$ do not [[consent]$_{Verb}$ [[to]$_{Prep}$ [[[PRO]$_{NP}$ [giving up these rights at any time]$_{VP}$]$_{S2}$]$_{NP}$]$_{PP}$]$_{VP}$]$_{S1}$

The bracketed structures in (3a–b) embody the assumption that there are two types of *to* in current English. The *to* in (3a) is under the Aux node (see for instance Chomsky 1981, 18–19). For this kind of *to*, linked to *to* infinitives, the term "infinitive marker" has been used in the literature. This label has sometimes been taken to mean that the *to* in question has no meaning, but the present author prefers to think that, similarly to other elements under the Aux node, infinitival *to* may carry a meaning. By contrast, the *to* of sentence (3b) is traditionally considered a preposition, and this view is adopted in this study. One reflex of a syntactic difference between the two types of *to* is that only the *to* under the Aux node permits VP Deletion, whereas prepositional *to* does not permit this (see Radford 1997, 53).[2] The contrast may be illustrated with the matrix verbs *try* and *resort*, featured above in (1a–b), which are predicates that only select one of the types of complement. There is thus a contrast between (4a) and (4b).

(4) a. Matt tried to use his fists, but his friend did not try to.
    b. *Matt resorted to using his fists, but his friend did not resort to.

In (4a) the word *to* is under the Aux node, and what follows *to* is a VP, as in structure (3a'). VP Deletion is therefore possible. By contrast, in (4b), analogously as in (3b'), what follows the word *to* is a nominal clause—that is, an NP dominating a sentence—not a VP, and, as a consequence, VP Deletion is out of the question.

In spite of the sharp syntactic difference between the two patterns, as illustrated in complements of *try* and *resort* in (4a–b), there are matrix verbs in English that have shown or continue to show variation between them, with *consent* being a case in point. The two patterns, of the types *John consented to do something* and *John consented to doing something*, are similar in that both involve subject control, with the covert lower subjects being controlled by the higher subjects. Further, the sense of the matrix verb *consent* seems similar in both cases, with the same sense of *consent* "Voluntarily to accede to or acquiesce in what another proposes or desires; to agree, comply, yield" (*OED*, sense 6a)[3] applicable to both usages. Chap. 2 begins with a brief survey of *to* infinitive and *to* -*ing* complements of *consent* in recent English, with data from the Corpus of

Historical American English, COHA. A more central objective is to provide information on the incidence of the two patterns in current British and American English. This is of added interest because the *OED* apparently does not illustrate the *to* -*ing* pattern in the entry for the verb at all.

Another major objective of Chap. 2 is to tease the two patterns apart from the point of view of the meanings of the two complementation patterns. This is not an easy task, but it is undertaken in the spirit of Bolinger's Principle. The verb *consent* is relatively rare today, but the American and British components of the GloWbE Corpus are of a sufficient size to be used as sources of data, providing the foundation of the investigation. The hypothesis put forward is termed the Choice Principle. Put briefly, this principle says that in the case of infinitival and gerundial complement options the former tends to be associated with agentive lower predicates and the latter with non-agentive lower predicates. The principle is defined and developed further in Chap. 2.

Chapter 3 takes up another predicate that has also shown variation between *to* infinitive and *to* -*ing* complements in recent times. This is the adjective *subject*. This adjective has a basic meaning of "Exposed or open to, prone to, or liable to suffer from something damaging, deleterious, or disadvantageous" (*OED*, sense 4a). It is commonly found with *to* NP complements, as in (5a), but it may also be found with sentential complements as in (5b). Both (5a) and (5b) are from COHA.

(5) a. ...you will be subject to the divine punishment you will have earned. (1981, FIC)
 b. ...he may be subject to being tried for this intentionally false plea or for perjury... (1946, MAG)

The chapter examines the incidence of the sentential complements of *subject* during the entire time span of COHA. In sentence (5b) the adjective selects a *to* -*ing* complement. By contrast a *to* infinitive complement would be less likely in a sentence such as (5b) today. However, it is observed, with evidence from COHA, that the adjective has also selected *to* infinitive complements in fairly recent English. The chapter sheds light on the incidence of the two types of sentential complements of the adjective in recent English. It also offers comments on the question of what may have contributed to the demise of the *to* infinitive pattern with the adjective *subject*.

Chapter 4 turns to variation between the *to* infinitive and a different gerundial pattern. Consider the sentences in (6a–b):

(6) a. I was ashamed to face them. (1945, COHA)
 b. ...I'm ashamed of telling you this,...(1959, COHA)

In both (6a) and (6b) the matrix adjective *ashamed* selects a sentential complement. The sentential complement in (6a) is a *to* infinitive and the gerundial complement in (6b) is what is labeled an *of -ing* complement, since the structure in question involves the preposition *of* and a following *-ing* clause. The chapter begins with comments on the meaning of the matrix adjective in the patterns of (6a–b), and then sheds light on the incidence of the two types of sentential complement in selected parts of COHA and COCA, the Corpus of Contemporary American English. A major purpose of the chapter is to investigate the question of whether the Choice Principle, introduced above in connection with contrasts between *to* infinitives and *to -ing* complements, might be applicable to account for variation between the *to* infinitive and the *of -ing* patterns selected by the adjective *ashamed*.

Chapter 5 turns from subject control to object control. For instance, consider sentence (7):

(7) ... we persuaded him to buy cigarettes for us,...(COHA 2000, MAG)

There are again two predications in sentence (7), and the lower clause is assumed to have its own subject, for instance, to ensure that its argument structure can be represented in a straightforward way. That subject is again PRO, but this subject is controlled by the higher object, not by the higher subject. The particular object control pattern investigated in Chap. 5 is what is termed the transitive *into -ing* pattern. An example is given in (8), from the Corpus of American Soap Operas.

(8) ... I pressured him into going along with me. (2000, AMC)

It has been noted in the literature that the transitive *into -ing* pattern can be used in innovative ways in current English, and the major purpose of the chapter is to explore its innovative uses in one particular type of scripted conversation, American soap operas. The corpus used, the Corpus of American Soap Operas, is approximately 100 million words in size. The corpus is large enough for the study of innovative usages in a particular text type, and these have not been investigated in the corpus before.

This book makes essential use of data from electronic corpora, and each chapter is largely based on one or more of the large corpora that Mark Davies of Brigham Young University has made available at his website. The scholarly community in the field of English owes a profound debt of gratitude to him for making it possible to investigate the grammar of English and grammatical variation in English with the help of such large and balanced corpora as COHA and COCA. The present book could not have been written without his corpora.

Here it is of interest to take note of a methodological point concerning work on complementation made by Leech et al. in their recent book:

> If we decide to focus on a specific non-finite complementation structure—such as, say, the *to*-infinitival clause or the gerund with possessive/genitive modifier—we will find these structures serving a large variety of functions, with most of them not being involved in current diachronic change. If, on the other hand, we decide to focus on more specific constructions—combinations of particular superordinate predicates and particular patterns of complementation (such as, for example, variation between infinitives and gerunds with *accustomed to*)—we can easily home in on areas of ongoing diachronic change, without, however, being able to correlate individual shifts in usage preferences with general trends in the evolution of the system of English non-finite verbal forms. (Leech et al. 2009, 181)

In most chapters of the book, the approach is what may be termed "head based," in that it proceeds from the investigation of "combinations of particular superordinate predicates and particular patterns of complementation." That is, it corresponds with the second approach outlined in the quotation above from Leech et al. (2009). It should be admitted that they are right to point out that in this approach the investigator may miss noticing "general trends." However, the investigator needs to start somewhere, and while no one investigator can hope to achieve in-depth studies of all the relevant matrix verbs, adjectives and nouns and their complementation patterns in order to provide a full picture of the trends of change and continuity, the present investigator harbors the hope that case studies of individual predicates and their complements can offer generalizations and predictions about other predicates and their complements, stimulating further work in the fascinating area of the system of English predicate complements. The present book has been written with the general aim of contributing to this research objective.

NOTES

1. While Rosenbaum (1967) is a pioneering work, it should also be noted that traditional grammarians made important contributions to the study of complementation. Pride of place among them belongs to H. Poutsma. His well-known grammar (Poutsma 1904, 1926) remains a valuable resource on complementation even today, but what is less well known today is that he also wrote a nearly complete draft of a comprehensive dictionary (Poutsma MS). The dictionary remains unpublished, but it is unique in the attention that it devotes to complementation and to variation in complementation. It is truly a treasure trove of information and an invaluable resource for the study of late nineteenth century and early twentieth century English, and it is used as an additional resource in the present book where appropriate.
2. Warner's (1993, 5, 64) analysis of infinitival *to* is similar in substance, but he argues that instead of VP Deletion the rule in question should be called "post-auxiliary ellipsis." Warner's argument deserves attention, but here the more established term "VP Deletion" is still used.
3. All references to the *OED* in this and later chapters, unless noted otherwise, are to the Online Edition of the *OED*, accessed in November 2015.

CHAPTER 2

Non-Finite Complements of the Verb *Consent* in Current American and British English

Abstract *To* infinitive complements of the verb *consent* are featured in standard sources of reference, including the *OED*, but it is shown in the chapter that the verb also selects *to -ing* complements. The chapter offers information on the incidence of the two types of non-finite complements in recent English, and then turns to the task of comparing the two from a semantic point of view. It is argued that this can be done with the help of the Choice Principle, which is based on the agentivity or otherwise of the sentential complement. The principle is seen to be statistically significant in predicting the selection of the type of complement in current English.

Keywords The Choice Principle · Subject control · Bolinger's Principle · Agentivity

2.1 Introduction

This chapter examines non-finite complements of the verb *consent* in current American and British English.[1] The *OED* is consulted here as a point of departure, because of its comprehensive coverage of complementation patterns in English. According to that dictionary, the verb has as many as nine senses, some of them with subsenses. However, only one of the nine senses appears to be current today. This is sense 6. Under 6a the following gloss is given in the *OED*:

> 6a. Voluntarily to accede to or acquiesce in what another proposes or desires; to agree, comply, yield. (*OED*)

Among the illustrations there are only two examples from later than 1700 that are sentential and non-finite. These are given in (1a–b):

(1) a. Argyle, after long resistance, consented...to divide his little army. (1849, T.B. Macaulay, *Hist. Eng.*)
 b. When I induce my creditor to consent to my paying a month hence. (1875, W.S. Jevons, *Money*)

In (1b) the complement of the matrix verb *consent* is a gerundial *-ing* clause, and it may be labeled an instance of the *Poss-ing* construction, but this pattern is set aside here, because the *-ing* clause has an expressed subject, and the present study focuses on sentential complements with covert subjects. On the other hand, sentence (1a) has a *to* infinitive complement. Given that the verb *consent* assigns a semantic role to its subject, the NP *Argyle* in (1a), the construction is clearly a control construction. More specifically, it is a subject control construction, with PRO controlled by the higher subject.

As regards other major dictionaries that pay close attention to complementation, Herbst et al. (2004) unfortunately does not include the verb at all. For their part, both the *Oxford Advanced Learner's Dictionary* (2005) and *Collins Cobuild Advanced Learner's Dictionary* (2003) of course include the verb and both feature the verb with *to* infinitive complements. However, only the latter mentions the possibility of a *to -ing* complement with the verb, and even that dictionary fails to give an illustration of the pattern. For its part, Poutsma's Dictionary (Poutsma MS), which is undated but was probably written in the 1930s, of course also has an entry for the verb. As far as subject control patterns are concerned, that dictionary, similarly to most of the other dictionaries, includes the *to* infinitive, which is illustrated for instance with *Mr. Brüning's resignation followed, though he has consented to carry on current business* (1932, *Times W*). The dictionary also includes this noteworthy comment: "There appears to be no alternative constructions with *to* + gerund" (Poutsma, MS).

This brief survey of earlier work may suggest that subject control constructions of *consent* do not offer a promising area for the investigation of grammatical variation. However, Rudanko (1996, 62) pointed to the possibility of *to -ing* complements with *consent* and in Rudanko (2012) he returned to them with more commentary, on the basis of data from American English. The present chapter is offered as a further contribution, with data from American English that have not been investigated before with respect to *consent*. A further extension concerns the consideration of data on *consent* from British English, allowing a first comparison of the *to -ing* and of the *to* infinitive patterns of the verb in the two main regional varieties of English.

2.2 Subject Control Complements of the Verb *Consent* in American and British English

The main purpose of this chapter is to investigate and to compare *to* infinitive and *to -ing* complements of the matrix verb *consent* in current American and British English, with data from the Corpus of Global Web-Based English, or the GloWbE Corpus or GloWbE, for short. However, as a preliminary it is of interest briefly to insert one or two remarks on the recent history of the two patterns in the last two centuries. COHA affords an opportunity to do so. It may be noted first that the verb *consent* has considerably declined in frequency in recent times. This can be shown for instance by the overall numbers of tokens for the 1870s and those for the 2000s. The former figure is 759 and the latter is only 74. These figures are obtained by the simple search string "[consent].[v*]." As for the frequencies of the two non-finite complementation patterns, they are of course much lower than these. The search strings "[consent].[v*] to [v?i*]" and "[consent]. [v*] to [v?g*]" can be used in this connection. They are not absolutely perfect in terms of recall (for recall and precision, see Ball 1994), given the possibility of insertions, but they are adequate enough to indicate historical trends. For the 1870s the search string for *to* infinitive complements retrieves as many as 352 tokens, and virtually all of these appear to be relevant. As for *to -ing* complements, their corresponding number is extremely low. The search string retrieves only four tokens, and one of these is irrelevant (*I consented to unsling my knapsack...* (1870, MAG, where the complement is of course a *to* infinitive), so that only three genuine examples remain. An example of each type is given in (2a–b):

(2) a. After considerable urging, he consented to go on terms so liberal. (1870, FIC)
 b. ...I may be the last man upon earth to consent to going into business with my wife. (1871, FIC)

In the 1870s the predominance of *to* infinitives over *to* -*ing* complements was thus overwhelming, with the ratio being in the region of 100 : 1. As for other decades of the nineteenth century, similar ratios obtain, or the ratios are even more strongly in favor of *to* infinitives. Setting the 1810s aside because the size of the subcorpus for that decade is small, it may be noted that no *to* -*ing* complements at all are found for the decades from the 1820s to the 1840s, while from the 1820 onwards, there are over 200 *to* infinitives in each decade, and for the 1850s there is only one *to* -*ing* complement, compared to almost 300 *to* infinitives.

Moving on from the nineteenth century, the verb itself becomes rarer, as do *to* infinitive complements. For instance, the search string retrieves 196 tokens for the 1910s. However, even though the verb becomes rarer, some tokens of *to* -*ing* are found in most decades of the twentieth century. For instance, there are three of them in the 1910s and four of them in the 1940s.

Turning to present-day English, the *to* infinitive continues to be much more frequent than the *to* -*ing* pattern even in current English. However, the ratios in favor of *to* infinitives over *to* -*ing* complements become somewhat less lopsided. In the three most frequent decades of COHA the numbers are 43 versus 3 for the 1980s (25.3 million words), 31 versus 1 for the 1990s (27.9 million words), and 28 versus 2 for the 2000s (29.6 million words). These figures are of interest in testifying to the existence of both subject control patterns in current English. However, the figures are far too low to be used as a basis for a comparative study of the two patterns and of factors that may affect variation between them in current English. For that, it is more helpful to turn to the American and British English segments of the GloWbE Corpus. This is done in the following.

The size of the American English segment of the GloWbE corpus is about 387 million words and that of the British English segment of the same corpus is almost precisely the same at about 388 million words.[2] These corpora are large enough to be suitable for investigating the nature of *to* infinitive and *to* -*ing* complements of the matrix verb *consent* in current English. As regards the American English segment, the search string used for *to* infinitives, which is again "[consent].[v*] to [v?i*]," retrieves 224 relevant tokens. It also retrieves a small number of irrelevant tokens, as in (3a–b).

(3) a. Consent to remain in the research should be obtained as soon as possible from the subject (wma.net)
    b. We do not consent to strip searches, virtual or otherwise. (ecommonsenseshow)

In (3a) the word *consent* is a noun, and as regards (3b) the word *consent* is a verb, but the following complement is a non-sentential *to* NP complement. Both types of sentences are excluded. The 224 relevant tokens translate to a normalized frequency of 0.6 per million words.

As for the *to -ing* pattern, the corresponding search string used is "[consent].[v*] to [v?g*]" and it yields 64 relevant tokens. This represents a normalized frequency of 0.2 for the *to -ing* pattern in the American English data. The numerical results obtained, 224 *to* infinitives and 64 *to -ing* complements, show that both types of complements can be found in the corpus in sizeable numbers. It is also of interest to note that the ratio in favor of the *to* infinitive in this large corpus of recent English is considerably less lopsided in the GloWbE Corpus than in the COHA data.

As regards the British English segment of the corpus, the corresponding search string for *to* infinitives retrieves 201 relevant tokens, and a small number of irrelevant tokens. The latter are largely of the same types as those in (3a–b). The normalized frequency of the relevant tokens is 0.5, which is slightly lower than the corresponding frequency in the American English segment. As for the *to -ing* pattern, the number of relevant tokens is 80, representing a normalized frequency of 0.2 in the British English data, approximating that of the American English data. In the absence of a corpus corresponding to COHA for British English, it is difficult to be sure about trends in British English, but the treatment of sentential complements of *consent* in the dictionaries surveyed above, especially in the *OED* and Poutsma (MS), suggests that *to -ing* complements were very rare with *consent* in nineteenth century British English.[3] It may then be possible to speak of a rising proportion of gerundial complements in relation to *to* infinitive complements. This trend would be in accordance a central feature of the Great Complement Shift (Rohdenburg 2006; see also Fanego 1996; Rudanko 2010b; and de Smet 2013). Further, British English does not appear to be lagging behind as regards this particular trend affecting the ratios of *to* infinitive and *to -ing* complements with the matrix verb *consent*.

2.3 Accounting for Grammatical Variation with the Verb *Consent* in Current American and British English

In Sect. 2.2 it was established that both *to* infinitive and *to -ing* complements occur with the matrix verb *consent* in current English, both in American and British English, in sizeable numbers when large corpora are consulted. This finding opens a research space for investigating principles that may affect the choice between them in current English. The focus is on testing the Choice Principle, which is a semantic principle for shedding light on the alternation between *to* infinitival and gerundial complements. This principle has been proposed very recently but its status cannot be regarded as established as yet. By contrast, the status of the Extraction Principle has been fully established by now in the relevant literature, and it is expedient first to inquire into the applicability of this principle in the present data.

A concise and clear definition of the Extraction Principle has been provided by Vosberg:

> In the case of infinitival or gerundial complement options, the infinitive will tend to be favoured in environments where a complement of the subordinate clause is extracted (by topicalization, relativization, comparativization, or interrogation etc.) from its original position and crosses clause boundaries. (Vosberg 2003a, 308)

In other work it has been pointed out that the extraction of adjuncts also deserves consideration from the point of view of the Extraction Principle (see Vosberg 2006, 63–67, Rohdenburg 2006; and Rudanko 2006, 43), but that does not reduce the appeal of the principle. When it is applied to the present data, it is observed that the overall number of extractions is relatively low, for instance in comparison to what has been observed in earlier work on the adjective *accustomed* (see Rudanko 2011, Chap. 6). In the American English subcorpus there are 15 extractions among the *to* infinitive and *to -ing* complements. Fifteen is a low number, but it is noteworthy that all 15 are found in the environments of *to* infinitive complements. This breakdown of the numbers is as expected on the basis of the Extraction Principle. Two examples are given in (4a–b), both of which involve Relativization.

(4) a. He had arranged for me to preach to his people, which I cheerfully consented to do. (docsouth)
 b. We are waiting for a concession speech from Romney which he has not consented to give. (care2)

In the British English data, the number of extractions is even lower, and only eight are found. Still the eight are again all found with *to* infinitive complements. Extraction data are thus seen to observe the Extraction Principle both in American and British English. Here are two illustrations from British English, again involving Relativization.

(5) a. ...some unique brilliance that the world would consent to call genius. (guardian.co.uk)
 ...a charge of assault arising out of a fight that the other consented to fight. (cirp.org)

Because of the established status of the Extraction Principle it can be taken for granted here without further discussion. The 15 plus 8 tokens that involve extraction in the present data are then set aside here, as being in accordance with the principle.

Turning now to the Choice Principle, the principle does not have the established status of the Extraction Principle, and a major purpose of the investigation is to find out whether it can shed light on the selection of sentential complements in the case of the tokens that do not involve an extraction. In the datasets considered here the number of such relevant infinitival tokens is 209 in the American English subcorpus and 193 in the British English subcorpus.

The Choice Principle has to do with the semantics of the lower predicate. A great deal has been written on the meaning of the *to* infinitive construction in English. Indeed, in the same article where he put forward his influential Generalization, Bolinger (1968, 125–127) offered some remarks on the meaning of *to* infinitives, comparing them with non-prepositional -*ing* complements. He observed that *to* infinitives tend to express something hypothetical, whereas -*ing* complements express something reified. Several other investigators have commented on the meanings of the two types of complements since Bolinger's important article, including Smith and

Escobedo (2001) and Smith (2009), but this investigation does not seek directly to derive an approach from the work of other scholars. Instead, the purpose is to examine whether a new approach, based on semantic roles, can be applied to *to* infinitive and *-ing* complements of *consent*. The approach was recently put forward in an analysis of the adjective *accustomed* in Rudanko (2010a) and Rudanko (2011, Chap. 6). In the case of the adjective *accustomed* the variation concerned *to* infinitives and *to -ing* complements of the adjective. In order to introduce the approach, consider the *to* infinitive complements in (6a–b), on the one hand, and the *to -ing* complements in (7a–b), from COHA, on the other:

(6) a. In former days folks were accustomed to exchange such rings at their betrothal ceremony. (1921, FIC)
 b. She was little accustomed to have her invitations, which she issued rather in the manner of royal commands, thus casually received. (1916, FIC)
(7) a. I am not accustomed to ordering my meals. (1918, FIC)
 b. Sir, I am not accustomed to having my word doubted. (1930, FIC)

The lower predicates in complements of *accustomed* in sentences (6a) and (7a) are *exchange such rings* and *ordering my meals*. These are similar in that they conceptualize acts or events as brought about by willful agents. In other words, the subjects of the lower clauses, which are implicit in (6a) and (7a), are agentive. The term "agentive" is here applied both to the semantic roles of the subjects and to the interpretations of the predicates selecting agentive subjects. In the analysis of agentivity it is helpful to recall Jackendoff's (1990, 126) notions of "doer of action," "volitional Actor," and "extrinsic instigator," which he set up in his discussion of "Actor–Patient relations." Further, it is helpful here to invoke the three notions of "volition, control, and responsibility" that come up in Hundt (2004, 49) as central elements of agentivity. (On control and controllability, see Berman 1970, 230 and Kuno 1970, 352.) A fully fledged Agent fulfills all three. Thus in (6a) and (7a) the referents of the subjects of the predicates *exchange such rings* and *ordering my meals* are conceptualized as exercising volition with respect to the actions designated by the predicates. The referents are further conceptualized as being in control of the actions and as being responsible for them.

In earlier work the term [+Choice] has been used to designate predicates that are agentive and their subjects, and the same terminology is adopted here. The terminology seems appropriate because "choice implies the exercise of volition and a volitional act" (Rudanko 2011, 133). It is also recalled that "volitional involvement in the event or state" may be considered as the key property of the "Agent Proto-Role" (Dowty 1991, 572). Applying Dowty's formulation, it is observed that the predicates *exchange such rings* and *order my meals* in their sentences in (6a) and (7a) express volitional involvement in an event. They encode the events in question as agentive, and the predicates and their subjects, as used in (6a) and (7a), are [+Choice].

By contrast, the lower predicates in complements of *accustomed* in (6b) and (7b) are of a different order. The lower predicate of (6b) is *have one's invitations thus casually received* and that of (7b) is *have one's word doubted*. These exemplify a construction of the type "*have* + NP + past participle." As noted in Rudanko (2012, 231), this construction can be causative, as in *He had all the prisoners punished* (from Palmer 1974, 199). In this case the construction is causative and the subject is agentive. However, it can also have a different interpretation, as for instance in *Alberto Tomba collided with a slalom pole and had his goggles knocked askew* (COCA 1992, cited in Rudanko 2015a, 22). The normal interpretation here is that the construction describes something that happened to the referent of the subject of the sentence, not an act or action in which the person was volitionally involved in, to hark back to Dowty's way of expressing the key property of agentivity. In Rudanko (2015a) the non-agentive interpretation of the construction is termed the "happenstance" reading, and the same term is used here. As used in sentences (6b) and (7b), the predicates *have one's invitations thus casually received* and *have one's word doubted* similarly do not encode "volitional involvement in the event or state," to quote Dowty (1991, 572) once more. Instead, they are of the happenstance *have* variety, and have a low degree of agentivity. They are therefore [−Choice], and their subjects are also [−Choice].

A useful way of shedding further light on the distinction between [+Choice] and [−Choice] predicates is also to consider imperatives. They are of interest here because they embody a property that has been well expressed by John R. Taylor:

> Prototypically, an imperative instructs a person to do something, and is therefore only acceptable if a person has a choice between carrying out the instruction or not. (Taylor 2003, 31)

To consider the lower predicates in sentences (6a) and (7a), it may be noted that imperatives of the type *Exchange such rings!* and *Order your meals!* are entirely natural, confirming the [+Choice] nature of these predicates. However, to consider the lower predicates in sentences (6b) and (7b), imperatives of the type *Have your invitations thus casually received!* and *Have your word doubted!* are much less likely, supporting the view that these predicates are [−Choice].

The sentences in (6a–b) show that no categorical rule can be given linking *to* infinitive to either [+Choice] or to [−Choice] readings, and the sentences in (7a–b) show that *-ing* complements cannot always be linked to either [+Choice] or [−Choice] readings either. However, in earlier work it has been argued that at a time of considerable variation between *to* infinitive and *-ing* complements selected by the same matrix adjective or verb, there is a significant tendency in the case of some matrix verbs and adjectives for *to* infinitives and [+Choice] readings to go together and for *-ing* complements and [−Choice] readings to go together (Rudanko 2011, Chap. 6). This generalization is here called the Choice Principle. It may be summed up as in the following:

The Choice Principle

In the case of infinitival and gerundial complement options at a time of considerable variation between the two patterns, the infinitive tends to be associated with [+Choice] contexts and the gerund with [−Choice] contexts.

The generalization about the impact of the Choice Principle was originally based on a study comparing *to* infinitive and *to -ing* complements of the adjective *accustomed* in Rudanko (2010a), and elaborated in Rudanko (2011, Chap. 6). It bears emphasizing that the Choice Principle is not a categorical rule. Instead it has been put forward as a tendency that may account for grammatical variation between *to* infinitival and gerundial complements at a time of variation between them.

The Choice Principle is thus based on the semantic role assigned by the lower predicate to the understood subject of the lower clause and it associates [+Choice] readings with *to* infinitive complements and [−Choice] readings with gerundial complements. These associations are not random, but may be related to what has been termed the forward-looking character of the relevant class of *to* infinitives. This means that the "action or state referred to in the infinitival clause follows the action or state referred to in the main clause" (Mair 1990, 102; cf. also Duffley's notion of "subsequence" in Duffley 2000, 224). A [+Choice] interpretation of the complement goes well with a forward-looking orientation, and while the present approach is original in being based on semantic roles, it can be linked to earlier work on the semantics of *to* infinitives. For their part, gerunds can sometimes be forward-looking, but they are less regularly so (Duffley 2000, 223), and more amenable to [−Choice] readings.

With the Choice Principle introduced and illustrated independently of *consent*, it is now possible to inquire into its application in the case of the two subject control variants selected by the verb. Beginning with the American English dataset, it is observed that sizeable numbers of both [+Choice] and [−Choice] lower predicates are found in the case of *to* infinitives and in the case of *to* -*ing* complements. The totals are given in Table 2.1.

Applying the Chi Square test to the data here, the Chi square is 11.2, and the results are significant at the <0.001 (df = 1) level of significance.

Two illustrations of *to* infinitives are given in (8a–b) and two illustrations of *to* -*ing* complements in (9a–b).

(8) a. After continuous pleading of his mother he consented to go to Lourdes. (olicway.blogspot)
 b. By closing the eyes and slumbering, and consenting to be deceived by shows, men establish and confirm their daily life of routine... (thoreau.eserve.org)
(9) a. ... the patient consented to paying the $600 cost. (blogs.nytimes.com)
 b. Would a TSO ever consent to having their own kids subjected to an "enhanced pat down"? (boardingarea.com)

Table 2.1 [+Choice] and [−Choice] lower predicates in *to* infinitive and *to* -*ing* complements of *consent* in the American English segment of the GloWbE Corpus

	[+Choice]	[−Choice]
to infinitive	142	67
to -*ing*	28	36

The lower predicates in sentences in (8a) and (9a) are [+Choice] in that *go to Lourdes* and *paying the $600 cost* convey volitional involvement on the part of the referents of their subjects in the actions in question. The notions of volition, control and responsibility are relevant to the conceptualizations of the events in question. By contrast, in (8b) and (9b) the predicates *be deceived by shows* and *having their own kids subjected to an "enhanced pat down"* are [−Choice]. The former is a passive, where the semantic role of the subject of the passive corresponds to, or is derivationally related to, the semantic role of the direct object of the active. The understood subject of the passive infinitive has the role of Patient, which is prototypically non-agentive and indeed at the opposite end from an Agent. As for the lower predicate of (9b), it represents an example of the happenstance *have* construction, with a similarly non-agentive lower subject.

Turning to the British English database, both [+Choice] and [−Choice] lower predicates are again found in both *to* infinitive and *to* -*ing* complements. The numerical findings are given in Table 2.2.

The Chi Square test may again be applied. The Chi square is 23.8, which is even higher than in the case of the American English data, and the results are significant at the <0.0001 level of significance (df = 1).

Illustrations of *to* infinitive complements are provided in (10a–b) and of *to* -*ing* complements in (11a–b).

(10) a. We would like to thank all patients and respondents who consented to participate in this study, ... (equityhealthj.com)
   b. ... those who responded to a survey or consented to be interviewed. (doceo.co.uk)
(11) a. ... they also have the capacity to consent to sharing their personal data with others ... (ico.gov.uk)
   b. ... he might not consent to being hit with a crow bar. (eversheds.com)

Table 2.2 [+Choice] and [−Choice] lower predicates in *to* infinitive and *to* -*ing* complements of *consent* in the British English segment of the GloWbE Corpus

	[+Choice]	[−Choice]
to infinitives	131	62
to -*ing*	28	52

Passives with Patient subjects are again prominent among [−Choice] lower predicates, as in (10b) and (11b).

The findings of the present study suggest that the Choice Principle is a factor affecting the choice of sentential complement with *consent* both in American and in British English. It also appears that the impact of the principle may be slightly stronger in British English than in American English. This regional difference is intriguing, but more of an invitation to further work than a confirmed result. On the other hand, the attraction of *to* -*ing* complements to [−Choice] predicates is observed in both regional varieties. This confirms earlier work on other predicates, including the adjective *accustomed*, that [−Choice] predicates have been a semantic niche through which gerundial complements have been able to spread.

In the current data [+Choice] lower predicates are likewise observed outside of their core area of *to* infinitive complements in sizeable numbers. It may well be that one reason for the relatively large number of such tokens of *to* -*ing* complements has to do with the Great Complement Shift. One of main features of the Shift is the general spread of gerundial complements at the expense of *to* infinitives, and this tendency may well be fostered by the kind of semantic niche observed in the previous paragraph. At the same time it is worth comparing the two patterns in the case of [+Choice] lower predicates further. Consider the authentic tokens of *to* -*ing* complements in (12a–c) and their invented *to* infinitive counterparts in (13a–c):

(12) a. Asked whether she would consent to removing her name from Rabbis for Obama, Rabbi Gottlieb told The Jewish Week: (gestetneupdates.com)
 b. He got her to answer that the mother, whom she referred to as "the primary caregiver," is the one who can consent to removing a baby against medical advice, rather than the father. (chappaqua.patchcom)
 c. But eventually he consented to cutting 54,916 words. (nytimes.com)

(13) a. Asked whether she would consent to remove her name from Rabbis for Obama, ...
 b. ...the mother...is the one who can consent to remove a baby against medical advice, ...
 c. But eventually he consented to cut 54,916 words.

Comparing such pairs, it is clear that alongside of the authentic tokens in (12a–c), the invented tokens in (13a–c) are also well formed and idiomatic. In each sentence the lower predicate is [+Choice], and the question is then whether a semantic difference can be discerned between the variants in such contexts.

In Rudanko (1996, 62) it was suggested that a complement of the *to -ing* type may place the predication of the lower clause at a further distance from the higher predication: "it is as if the action or activity expressed by the lower clause were at a further remove from the constituents of the matrix clause." As far as the sentences in (12a–c) and (13a–c) are concerned, it may be possible to make a more specific suggestion about what distance may mean and relate the idea of distance to the notion of control. That is, the notion of straightforward or strict subject control seems more relevant to the *to* infinitive variants, whereas in the case of the *to -ing* complements there is more scope for PRO to be less closely or less directly bound in its reference to the higher subject. For instance (12b) seems amenable to the interpretation that maybe someone other than the mother would remove a baby against medical advice and in (12c) the actual cutting might be done by someone other than the referent of *he*, with the other person observing the instructions of the referent of the higher subject. If this suggestion is on the right lines, it would invoke one of the properties of gerunds that has been observed independently for other predicates (see for instance Allerton 1988, 15–16). That said, it must be added that the difference in control does not always surface in this way. For instance, consider the sentences in (14a–b), again with [+Choice] lower predicates:

(14)   a. ...the European Court of Human Rights requires that the individual who consents to waiving his fundamental rights does so in an explicit manner. (law.ed.ac.uk)
       b. ...you cannot complain as the women consented to getting married to the Man knowing full well he is already married. (ummah.com)

In (14a–b) it is hard to interpret the lower subject as involving anything other than straightforward or strict subject control. The idea of distance may still be applicable though, with the sense of the key part of (14a), for instance, being close to "the individual who consents to the idea of waiving his fundamental rights," but this comment is more of an invitation to further work on teasing the two patterns apart in this case than a confirmed finding.

2.4 Concluding Observations

The verb *consent* is not very frequent in current English, but it is not obsolete, and as far as its sentential complements are concerned, most major dictionaries feature the verb as selecting *to* infinitive complements. Such complements were clearly frequent with the verb in the nineteenth century. As for *to -ing* complements, they were very rare, even to the extent that Poutsma (MS) suggested that they were not found at all. However, this chapter shows that even though the verb is relatively rare today, it currently selects both *to* infinitives and *to -ing* complements in both American and British English.

A central theme of this chapter concerns the task of identifying the factors that bear on the selection of the two types of non-finite complements. The Extraction Principle is considered as an established generalization, but in the present data extractions are quite rare. Nevertheless the Extraction Principle is of interest, for extractions are linked to *to* infinitive complements in both the American English and British English datasets.

The main focus of the chapter is on the Choice Principle. This principle was found to be supported both by the large American English and British English datasets considered in the chapter. As predicted by the generalization, in both regional varieties [+Choice] lower predicates tend to go with *to* infinitive complements, and for their part [−Choice] lower predicates are linked to *to -ing* complements. This is the main finding of the chapter, but it also offers some more speculative suggestions on tokens where *to -ing* complements are found with [+Choice] lower predicates. *To* infinitives are well formed alternatives for them, but it is suggested that the *to -ing* variants may involve more distance between the higher and the lower predications and that sometimes the notion of distance may be amenable to being interpreted as embodying a difference in control properties.

Notes

1. Rudanko (2012, 229–231) contains a brief discussion of *consent*, based on data from COCA. The current chapter is meant to offer a fuller discussion of the verb. This study is based on different corpora, partly to see if the results

of the earlier study are confirmed in such other corpora. Further, the current study compares current usage in American English with current usage in British English, which was not within the scope of the earlier investigation.
2. The GloWbE Corpus is aggregative, and there is lack of information about individual speakers whose language is included in the corpus (see Brezina and Meyerhoff 2014 on using aggregate data and Mukherjee 2015 on using GloWbE specifically). What recommends using this corpus here is its size. Further, the presence of blogs in the corpus may reveal clues about very recent trends in the use of English.
3. There is no corpus corresponding to COHA for British English presently available, but the third part of the Corpus of Late Modern English Texts gives some indication of the incidence of the two types of complements with *consent* in the text type of fiction in the period from 1850 to 1920. It turns out that there are 178 tokens of *to* infinitive complements of *consent* in that corpus, and only one *to -ing* complement. This finding broadly confirms Poutsma's intuition about the rarity of *to -ing* complements in that period.

CHAPTER 3

Non-Finite Complements of the Adjective *Subject* in Recent American English

Abstract The adjective *subject* is often thought of as selecting *to* NP complements in English, as in *The area is subject to earthquakes*. However, it is pointed out that the adjective has also selected sentential complements, both *to* infinitives and *to* -*ing* complements, in the last two centuries. The chapter investigates the trajectories of these types of sentential complement in recent English, and offers a hypothesis for understanding the near demise of the *to* infinitive complement with the adjective. Comments are also included on the disassociation of infinitival *to* from prepositional *to*.

Keywords Subject control · The Choice Principle · Infinitival *to* · Prepositional *to* · The Great Complement Shift

3.1 INTRODUCTION

This chapter investigates non-finite complements of the adjective *subject* in recent English. The *OED* analysis of the senses of the adjective is comprehensive, containing as many as ten senses, with plentiful illustrations. Rather than giving a full survey of the numerous senses and the various patterns found with them, it is more appropriate here to focus on the complementation patterns that are directly relevant. With the focus of the present book on non-finite complements, it is observed that examples of *to* infinitives are found under sense 1c "Under obligation, bound (formerly

© The Author(s) 2017
J. Rudanko, *Infinitives and Gerunds in Recent English*,
DOI 10.1007/978-3-319-46313-1_3

also †compelled) *to* do something. Now *rare*." The two most recent illustrations of these are given in (1a–b).

1. a. ...every merchant should be subject to give the information...
       (1862, House of Commons)
    b. Both corporations and individuals are subject to pay income tax in the US. (1998, C. Rossini., *Eng. as Legal Lang.*)

To infinitive complements are also found under sense 7 of the adjective "Having a tendency *to* do something. Formerly also: †prone, or disposed *to* an action (*obs.*). Now *rare*." The two most recent illustrations under this sense are given in (2a–b).

(2) a. Potash glass is less subject to crack. (1854, J. Scoffern, *Orr's Circ. Sc.*)
    b. As an urban teen in America, I was subject to become a victim of all those social ills. (2009, A. J. Gunn, *Audacity of Leadership*)

In the *OED* there do not appear to be any *to* -*ing* complements among the plentiful illustrations of the adjective. As far as the *Oxford Advanced Learner's Dictionary* (2005) is concerned, there are illustrations of *to* NP complements but no sentential complements featured with the adjective. Neither does the *Collins Cobuild Dictionary* (2003) feature non-finite complements with it. On the other hand, *to* NP complements are featured, and two helpful senses are given for the adjective. The first, illustrated for instance with *In addition, interest on Treasury issues isn't subject to state and local income taxes*, is given as follows "To be **subject** to something means to be affected by it or to be likely to be affected by it." The second meaning of the adjective in the *Collins Cobuild Dictionary* has more narrowly to do with rules or laws: "If someone is subject to a particular set of rules or laws, they have to obey those rules or laws." This sense is illustrated with *The tribunal is unique because Mr Jones is not subject to the normal police discipline rules*.

For its part, while Poutsma (MS) gives numerous examples of *to* NP complements, he also points to an example of what here is called a *to* -*ing* complement. This is reproduced in (3).

(3) He has been subject to talking and starting. (Congreve, *Love for Love*)

The solitary illustration is of interest, but it is from a fairly old source and by itself the one example only invites further investigation.

It is the purpose of this chapter to investigate *to* infinitive and *to* -*ing* complements of the adjective *subject* with the help of COHA. The investigation is undertaken against the background of the Choice Principle, which was put forward in Chap. 2. The adjective is of particular interest in the context of the Choice Principle because of the semantics of the adjective. The definitions of the senses of the adjective are not identical in the major dictionaries surveyed above, but definitions contain elements such as "under obligation...to do something" or "to be affected by something." Language such as "under obligation" (under sense 1c in the *OED*) or "to be affected" (the broader sense in *Collins Cobuild*) suggests that the adjective may be associated with an event being conceptualized non-agentively. That is, in this interpretation the referent of the subject of the lower clause embedded under the adjective is not conceived as being volitionally involved in the action or event in question. The interpretation would then be expected to be [−Choice]. Further, while language such as "disposed to an action" or "having a tendency to do something," prominent in one of the senses in the *OED*, does not necessarily suggest a [−Choice] interpretation, the most recent illustrations of the sense in the *OED*, given in (2a–b), involve lower predicates of the [−Choice] variety. Recalling the Choice Principle given in Chap. 2, the meaning of the adjective *subject* therefore leads to the expectation that the complementation of the adjective might be a fertile ground for the *to* -*ing* pattern to emerge and to prosper, in the context of the Great Complement Shift (see Chap. 2). COHA affords a large enough corpus to investigate whether this expectation is borne out.

3.2   Non-Finite Complements of the Adjective *Subject* in COHA

To search for tokens of *to* infinitives of the adjective *subject* in COHA the search string "subject to [v?i*]" suggests itself, and the corresponding search string for *to* -*ing* complements is "subject to [v?g*]." The search strings retrieve a fairly large number of irrelevant tokens, as in (4a–b) for *to* infinitives and (5a–b) for *to* -*ing* complements:

(4) a. ...I was glad to have a subject to employ my thoughts...(1835, FIC)

b. Let me hope that I have said enough upon the subject to suggest thoughts, which those who take an interest in it may pursue... (1852, NF)
(5) a. Mr. Miller had been subject to fainting spells recently. (1911, NEWS)
b. On the basis of their higher earnings the hotels are subject to rising Federal income levies. (1943, NEWS)

In both of (4a–b) the word *subject* is of course a noun, and such tokens are irrelevant and set aside. As for (5a–b), the word is an adjective in them, but it is followed by a *to* NP complement.

The search strings employed reveal that both *to* infinitive and *to -ing* complements have been found with the adjective *subject* in recent times, though their frequency is not very high. The frequencies for each decade of COHA are given in Table 3.1.

Table 3.1 Frequencies of *to* infinitive and *to -ing* complements of the adjective *subject* in the different decades of COHA

Decade	to *infinitives*	to -ing *complements*
1810s	0	1
1820s	3	0
1830s	8	0
1840s	12	3
1850s	6	1
1860s	5	0
1870	3	1
1880s	3	0
1890s	3	1
1900s	1	0
1910s	0	0
1920s	1	2
1930s	3	1
1940s	1	5
1950s	0	1
1960s	0	4
1970s	0	3
1980s	1	4
1990s	0	3
2000s	0	1

Some illustrations of the two types of non-finite complements from the two centuries are given in (6a–d) and (7a–d).

(6) a. ...the oak is seldom straight grained, and very subject to warp. (1827, NF)
  b. ...leaves the mass of whites comparatively uninformed, and peculiarly subject to be deceived and misled,...(1862, MAG)
  c. ...we find the other Wheat is subject to be destroyed in the Fall by Wheat-lice,...(1934, NF)
  d. It [Bavarian Red Liquor] renders the Face delightfully handsome and beautiful, is not subject to be rubbed off like paint...(1980, FIC)

(7) a. A man who might be afraid to defeat a law by his single veto, might not scruple to return it for reconsideration; subject to being finally rejected, only in the event of more than one third of each house concurring in the sufficiency of his objections. (1817, NF)
  b. ...he should have a pet, which should be all his own, and subject to fondling by no other hands;...(1875, FIC)
  c. ...writers who were not war correspondents and who therefore were not subject to having their copy examined before it was printed;...1946, MAG)
  d. A side constraint determines directly what ought to be done; it is not subject to being weighed against other reasons. (1999, NF)

The information about the frequencies of the two types of non-finite complements in Table 3.1 shows that as far as these complements of the adjective *subject* are concerned, there was a strong preference for the *to* infinitive over the *to* -*ing* pattern in the nineteenth century. Further, it is observed in Table 3.1 that the frequencies of *to* infinitives were at their highest in the decades from the 1830s to the 1850s and the 1860s, after which their frequencies began to decline. In the course of the twentieth century the preference for *to* infinitives was clearly reversed, and the *to* -*ing* complement became much more frequent than the *to* infinitive. The reversal did not happen overnight, and it was only from the 1940s onwards that it became more definite. For the sake of convenience and to represent the overall trend, it is perhaps appropriate here to compare the two centuries. This is done in Table 3.2.

Table 3.2 *To* infinitive and *to* -*ing* complements of the adjective *subject* in the nineteenth and twentieth centuries

	to *infinitives*	to -ing *complements*
Nineteenth century	43	7
Twentieth century	7	24

Applying the Chi square test, the Chi square is as high as 29.95, and the difference is significant at the level of <0.001 (df = 1). This investigation therefore shows that while both *to* infinitives and *to* -*ing* complements are found with the adjective *subject* in recent English, the former predominated in the nineteenth century and that there has been a definite shift favoring the *to* -*ing* construction over the *to* infinitive in twentieth-century English. This finding is in accordance with the expectation set up on the basis of the Great Complement Shift and the semantics of the adjective, as discussed in Sect. 3.1.

The data of the two non-finite complementation patterns retrieved from COHA make it possible to probe the salience of the Choice Principle in relation to the semantic analysis of the adjective *subject* a little further. As a preliminary it may be noted that as far as extractions are concerned, their salience is the present datasets is minimal, for there is only one of them found. This is given in (8).

(8) ...when seed is sown in the fall, it should be on a piece of ground where it is not subject to be inundated or covered with water, which rots the seed in the ground, and is an almost sure cause of failure;... (1839, FIC)

Where in sentence (8) may be linked to a gap in the sentential complement of the adjective *subject*, and the complement is a *to* infinitive, as may be expected, but it is the only example of an extraction in the data, and the example is set aside when the Choice Principle is considered.

Turning to the remaining tokens, eight examples of the adjective with non-finite complements were given in (6a–d) and (7a–d), and it is striking that all of them involve lower predicates that are [–Choice]. In five of the eight the lower predicates are passives, either passive *to* infinitives or passive -*ing* forms, and in their case the lower subject has a prototypically non-agentive interpretation, as was pointed out in Chap. 2.

As for sentence (7c), the lower predicate is of the syntactic type "have NP past participle," and involves a happenstance interpretation, which is also non-agentive, as was noted in Chap. 2. This leaves us with examples (6a) and (7b). The former is about an oak warping, which is [−Choice] since the question of volitional involvement does not arise in the case of an oak. As for the latter, it is of the type *His pet should be subject to fondling by no other hands*. The verb *fondle* is often used agentively, as in *He bent to the puppy, fondled her soft brown ear*... (COHA, 1994, FIC), but in (7b) the complement of *subject* is interpreted non-agentively, in the manner of "subject to being fondled" (compare the category of "concealed passives" in Huddleston and Pullum 2002, 1199–2000). The passive interpretation of *fondling* is also confirmed by the following *by* phrase.

It turns out that in the data of both *to* infinitives and of *to -ing* complements there is a strong tendency for lower predicates embedded under the adjective *subject* to be non-agentive, as in the examples in (6a–d) and (7a–d). Passive lower clauses were seen to be very prominent in (6a–d) and (7a–d), and they are also very prominent in the rest of data. For example, the 1840s may be considered. It was during this decade that the highest number of non-finite tokens of either type were found, with the number of *to* infinitives reaching 12. What is striking is that in as many as ten of the 12 the lower clause is in the passive. Two examples are given in (9a–b), both from magazines, but different ones.

(9) a. It is a law, no doubt, subject to be referred to erroneous applications, to justify what cannot be justified...(1841, MAG)
 b. Are the rights held as civil rights bestowed by a law, and subject to be taken away by its repeal—or as property, lands, for instance, under a formal conveyance. (1841, MAG)

As noted, in examples of the type of (9a–b) the lower predicates are of the [−Choice] variety. It is clear from the abundance of examples such as (9a–b) in the 1840s that the *to* infinitive was very well suited to [−Choice] contexts at that time.

As for any possible counterexamples to the predominance of non-agentive lower predicates, they are very rare. The examples in (10a–c) are worth considering in this context.

(10) a. "All of us, my honest friend," continued the Doctor, "are subject to making mistakes; so the chief art of life, is to know to best to remedy mistakes." (1925, FIC)
b. You can't manufacture the good night's sleep and sell it with the bed. But, still, it is something to know the sleep would be a good one, and that the man responsible for it is quite a bit like yourself. Middle-aged, paunchy, and often subject to lying awake. (1952, FIC)
c. ...about $179 million in annual gas revenues now being collected under more than 3300 pending interstate contracts is being held in escrow, with producers subject to making refunds, plus 6 % interest, for any portion of charges not approved in the F.A.C.'s final decision in each case. (1961, NEWS)

As regards (10a), the predicate *make mistakes* can be used agentively, for one can make a mistake deliberately, but the context of (10a) suggests making mistakes inadvertently. Similarly, while it is possible to lie awake deliberately, the context of sentence (10b) again suggests a context of involuntary insomnia and lying awake as not being conceived of as something volitional. For its part sentence, (10c) is perhaps the most interesting of these putative counterexamples to non-agentive lower predicates. The predicate *make refunds* is certainly agentive and [+Choice] as normally used, and it may be too bold to deny its agentive status even in (10c). Nevertheless, in sentence (10c) the construction *subject to making refunds* seems close in meaning to *subject to having to make refunds*, which suggests overtones of non-agentivity, emanating from the adjective *subject*, even in the case of a lower predicate that is normally [+Choice]. If this is so, the term "non-agentive reinterpretation" might be used for this type of coercion.

Even setting non-agentive reinterpretations aside, over 90 % of lower predicates in both *to* infinitives and *to -ing* complements are clearly of the non-agentive type in the datasets. Seen against this background, the change in the complementation of the adjective *subject*—from *to* infinitives to *to -ing* complements—is not random, but can be accounted for in part on the basis of the Choice Principle, in the general context of the Great Complement Shift. (For discussion of the Great Complement Shift, see Rohdenburg 2006). The adjective *subject* can select non-finite complements, and when it does, its meaning is such that it favors lower clauses of the [–Choice] type. Since *-ing* complements, including *to -ing* complements, are associated with such interpretations, it is only natural that non-finite complements of the adjective have gravitated towards that type of complement, at the expense of *to* infinitives.

What is also of further interest is the finding that *to* infinitives were very compatible with [−Choice] complements of the adjective *subject* in the nineteenth century. It is recalled for instance that in the 1840s there were 12 *to* infinitive complements of the adjective and of the 12 ten were in the passive. As noted, such passives have prototypically [−Choice] interpretations. This finding, together with the finding that *to* infinitives become very rare as complements of the adjective in the course of the twentieth century suggests that there may have been a change in the interpretation of the *to* infinitive in the course of the last two centuries.

To shed some further light on the nature of the change affecting *subject*, it is of interest to refer back to the argument used at the beginning of Chap. 1 to justify the analysis that infinitival *to* should be placed under the Aux node in current English. That argument was based on VP Deletion, or its interpretive analogue, to account for sentences of the type of *Matt tried to use his fists, but his friend did not try to*, as compared with the ill-formedness of *to -ing* complements not permitting corresponding constructions, as in **Matt resorted to using his fists, but his friend did not resort to*. The reason for bringing up this argument in the context of the findings relating to the non-finite complements of the adjective *subject* is that the availability of VP Deletion sentences in current English has been recognized to be a fairly recent phenomenon in that in the early nineteenth century such examples were very rare. Denison (1998, 201) discusses the type of ellipsis in question, with an example from the *OED*, given here as (11).

(11) that if every one of your clients is to force us to keep a clerk, whether we want to or not, you had better leave off business…(1840, Dickens, *Old Curiosity Shop*)

Denison comments on the history of the type of VP ellipsis in question, noting that "until the mid-nineteenth century and after most writers avoided it" (1998, 201; see also Warner 1993, 64). He goes on: "From then on, however, what had been a trickle soon turned into a flood" (Denison 1998, 201).

COHA gives further evidence in favor of Denison's point. A full investigation of the issue cannot be undertaken here, but even an inquiry into the construction with the one matrix verb *want*, chosen in view of Denison's example and because the verb frequently occurs with VP Deletion in current English, yields interesting findings. COHA permits searches that make reference to commas and periods. Such environments do not of course give perfect recall, but they are typical of VP Deletion contexts, and they may suffice here to shed light on historical trends. When searches are conducted for search strings consisting of the verb *want* and the word *to* immediately followed by a comma or a period during the period from the 1810s to the 1880s, the results given in Table 3.3 are obtained, with the normalized frequencies given in parentheses.

The figures in Table 3.3 reveal a dramatic rise in the frequency of the VP Deletion construction within a short space of time, especially during the period from the 1830s and 1840s to the 1860s. Three examples from the early decades of the corpus are given in (12a–c):

(12) a. ... if I could ever pay a compliment in my life, when I wanted to. (1823, FIC)
 b. "Why didn't she come?" "Well—I believe she didn't want to," said Mr. Allen. (1845, FIC)
 c. "Do you often go out alone so late?" "Whenever I want to." (1852, FIC)

The emergence of VP Deletion constructions with *to* infinitives indicates a major stage in what Denison has called the "drift of the English infinitive from a nominal to a verbal character, now virtually complete, and the concomitant disassociation of the infinitive marker *to* from the homonymous preposition" (Denison 1998, 266). The change in question, it may be proposed, created a fertile ground for the spread of the *to* *-ing* pattern with the adjective, where the *to* *-ing* complement, which involves a gerund, is more nominal than a *to* infinitive complement[1] and more readily able to be associated with a characteristic [−Choice] flavor. Since the meaning of the adjective *subject* favors such complements, the change in favor of the *to* *-ing* pattern was the natural consequence.

To supplement the discussion that has been based on COHA so far, it is also of interest to consider the United States segment of the GloWbE corpus. As noted in Chap. 2, this subcorpus is about 387 million words in size, and it affords an opportunity to deepen our understanding of the nature of the non-finite complements of the adjective *subject* in current American English. The same search strings as were used in the case of COHA were employed, and they yield 22 *to* infinitive complements and 170 *to* *-ing* complements of the

Table 3.3 The verb *want* followed by a comma or a period in COHA from the 1810s to the 1880s

Decade	No. of tokens
1810s	0
1820s	3 (0.4)[a]
1830s	5 (0.4)
1840s	19 (1.2)
1850s	39 (2.4)
1860s	115 (6.7)
1870s	137 (7.4)
1880s	159 (7.8)

Note: [a] Normalized frequencies given in parentheses

adjective. These overall figures confirm the overall preponderance of the *to -ing* construction over the *to* infinitive pattern with the adjective today.

The overwhelming majority of the 192 non-finite complements contain lower predicates that are [−Choice]. Their number is 172. To consider the 170 *to -ing* complements first, 150 are [−Choice], and 20 are [+Choice]. Some examples of the former type, taken from among these complements, are given in (13a–c)

(13) a. When on another person's premises, visitors are subject to being watched. (mises.org)
 b. Even people with so-called "private" settings are subject to having their public name and profile image used and re-used. (businesspundit.com)
 c. Testing premises are subject to videotaping. (ets.org)

The examples in (13a–c) illustrate different types of [−Choice] lower predicates. The lower predicate in example (13a) is a straightforward passive, and given earlier comments on such passives, it does not need further comment at this point. In sentence (13b) the lower predicate is of the type "*have* NP Past Participle." As was noted in Chap. 2, the construction can have a causative [+Choice] reading, but in (13b it is of the happenstance *have* variety, conveying what happens to the referent of the understood subject of the lower clause. As for sentence (13c), the lower predicate has a passive interpretation, similarly to the example *subject to fondling by other hands,* noted above in example (7b), which is interpreted as "subject to being fondled." In the case of (13c) the interpretation is "subject to being videotaped." Passive interpretations of *-ing* forms that lack the passive morphology are quite frequent among the *to -ing* complements of *subject* in the present data, and 44 of the 170 *to -ing* complements of the adjective are of this type.

Regarding the 20 [+Choice] *to -ing* complements in the dataset, one or two are tokens where it is not clear that they involve subject control in the first place. An example is in (14).

(14) Not everything should be subject to thinking about the next election instead of thinking about the next generation. (thehill.com)

The remaining [+Choice] lower predicates may be regarded as involving what were termed non-agentive reinterpretations above, involving overtones of non-agentivity, as in sentence (10c) above. For instance, consider (15a–b):

(15) a. If you have a profit of more than $400, you would be subject to paying social security and medicare taxes on that amount. (financialplanning.org)
b ...they would be free to leave the organization (subject to complying with existing commitments they have made)... (marketingland. com)

Overall, there is a strong tendency for lower predicates to be [–Choice] in the present dataset, and this is in accordance with the finding made on the basis of data from COHA above.

Turning to the 22 *to* infinitive complements, they show that *to* infinitives are not totally extinct with the adjective *subject* in current English. The tokens are also [–Choice] as regards their interpretations, apparently without an exception. Three illustrations are given in (16a–c):

(16) a. No person shall be subject to be twice put in jeopardy for the same offense,... ((leg.state.nv.us)

b. ...all corporations shall have the right to sue and shall be subject to be sued, in all courts, in like cases as natural persons. (leg.wa.gov.)
c. They go, however, with more certainty than the others, who are subject to be misled in their intellectual illuminations; but these are guided by a supreme Will which conducts them howsoever it will. (passtheword.org)

The frequency of *to* infinitive complements with the adjective *subject* is a fraction of *to* -*ing* complements in the United States segment of the GloWbE dataset. To judge by the data of the corpus, it appears that the explanation for their incidence may be sought in the text types in which they occur. The examples in (16a–b) are from legal English and that of (16c) is from religious usage. Both of these are formal and conservative text types, and the present investigation suggests that in them *to* infinitive complements are surviving longer than in other text types considered.

3.3 Concluding Observations

The chapter focuses on *to* infinitive and *to* -*ing* complements of the adjective *subject* in the last two centuries. Data from COHA reveal that in nineteenth-century American English there was a pronounced preference for *to* infinitives, with 43 *to* infinitives compared to only 7 *to* -*ing* complements. In the course of the twentieth century *to* -*ing* complements were found to become noticeably more frequent in relation to *to* infinitives, to the extent that there is today a very marked preponderance of *to* -*ing* complements over *to* infinitives. It was noted that a prominent sense of the adjective has to do with obligation or the notion of being affected (by something or someone), and it was argued that such notions go naturally with [−Choice] interpretations of sentential complements. From this perspective the overall change in the sentential complements of the adjective may then be explicable on the basis of the Choice Principle.

It was also suggested, with respect to the general predominance of *to* infinitive complements in relation to *to* -*ing* complements even with [−Choice] lower predicates in the early and middle part of the nineteenth century, that the predominance may be linked to the nature of the word *to* at that time. In current English infinitival *to* is clearly distinct from the preposition *to*, and a strong argument for the distinction has to do with the ability of infinitival *to* to allow VP Deletion. However, as noted by Denison (1998), the type of VP Deletion in question only became frequent from about the 1850s onwards. It may then be speculated that prior to that time, infinitival *to* was less clearly distinct from prepositional *to*. In other words, prior to the spreading of VP Deletion in the case of *to* infinitive complements the process that Denison (1998, 266) called the "drift of the English infinitive from a nominal to a verbal character" was at a considerably less advanced stage. That is, *to* infinitives at that less advanced stage of the process were still more nominal in character than what they became after the middle of the nineteenth century. This may explain why it was easier at that earlier stage for *to* infinitives to involve [−Choice] lower predicates than after infinitival *to* became more verbal in nature.

The chapter concluded with consideration of data from the American English segment of the GloWbE corpus. Overall, data from that corpus confirmed that sentential complements of the adjective *subject* tend to be linked to [−Choice] complements and that among such complements in current English *to -ing* complements are much more frequent than *to* infinitives. At the same time, the study of this corpus also revealed that *to* infinitive complements are still easily found with the adjective in legal and religious English, which may be viewed as conservative text types.

This chapter naturally invites further work on the grammatical status of infinitival *to* in the nineteenth century. Further, it invites further work on the recent history of the adjective *subject* in other regional varieties of English, and the question of the potential influence of text type on complement selection also merits further attention.

NOTE

1. See Ross (2004) for a full discussion of a hierarchy of nouniness or sententiality among different types of complements, including *to* infinitives and *ing* clauses.

CHAPTER 4

The Semantics of *to* Infinitives and *of-ing* Complements: A Case Study on the Adjective *Ashamed*

Abstract Noting that the adjective *ashamed* selects both *to* infinitive and *of-ing* complements, this chapter investigates the relevance of the Choice Principle to complement selection in the case of this adjective. The principle was introduced in Chap. 2 to separate *to* infinitive and gerundial complements, and it is based on a distinction in the semantic interpretation of the two types of sentential complements. The principle is applied to large bodies of data from the Corpus of Historical American English and from the Corpus of Contemporary American English. It is argued that the principle is a factor with a significant impact on the complement selection properties of the adjective *ashamed*. More broadly, the principle also serves to shed light on the semantic interpretation of *to* infinitive and gerundial complements in recent English.

Keywords The Choice principle · *To* infinitives · The preposition *of* · The hinge construction

4.1 Introduction

Consider the sentences in (1a–b):

(1) a. I was ashamed to face them. (1945, COHA)
     b. ... I'm ashamed of telling you this, ... (1959, COHA)

The sentences in (1a–b) are similar in that in each of them the matrix predicate is the adjective *ashamed* and in that in each the adjective selects a sentential complement.[1] It is assumed here, in view of the arguments in Chap. 1, that in each case the lower clause has its own understood or implicit subject. As regards the subject of the matrix predicate *ashamed* in (1a–b), it is assigned a theta role by the adjective *ashamed* in both of (1a–b), which means that both sentences are control constructions. Given that both sentences are control structures, the symbol PRO may then again be used to represent the understood subjects of the two sentences. The sentential complement of *ashamed* in sentence (1a) is obviously a *to* infinitive clause, and the sentential complement of the adjective in sentence (1b) is here called an *of-ing* complement. In the latter case the *-ing* clause is a gerund, to use a traditional label.

Minimal representations of the key parts of the two sentences are given in (1a′) and (1b′):

(1) a′. [[he]$_{NP1}$ was [ashamed]$_{Adj}$ [[PRO]$_{NP2}$ [to]$_{Infl}$ [face them]$_{VP}$]$_{S2}$]$_{S1}$
 b′. [[I]$_{NP1}$ am [ashamed]$_{Adj}$ [[of]$_{Prep}$ [[[PRO]$_{NP2}$ [telling you this]$_{VP}$]$_{S2}$]$_{NP}$]$_{PP}$]$_{S1}$

The structure in (1a′) is in accordance with the analysis in Chomsky (1981, 18–19) in that infinitival *to* is placed under the Infl node, corresponding to the more traditional label of Aux. As for (1b′), it makes use of the traditional notion of nominal clause in that the lower S node is dominated by an NP node. This is in accordance with the status of the lower clause as a gerund.

The meanings of the two patterns when selected by the adjective *ashamed* are fairly close, and there are major dictionaries where *to* infinitives and *of* complements of the adjective are treated under the same sense, without being distinguished with respect to their meanings. For instance, the third edition of the *OALD* (1979), while not specifically separating *of-ing* complements from *of* NP complements, has this entry for the adjective *ashamed*, leaving out the information about its pronunciation:

> ashamed ... *pred adj*—(*of/that/to do sth*), feeling shame: *You should be— of yourself/of what you have done. He was/felt—to ask for help. He felt—that*

he had done/of having done so little. I feel—for you, on your account, as if I were you. (*OALD* 1979, s.v.)

On the other hand, the *OED*, while also not specifically distinguishing *of-ing* complements from other complements introduced by the preposition *of*, offers two relevant senses for the adjective. Sense 1 is defined in part as follows:

1. Affected with shame; abashed or put to confusion by a consciousness of guilt or error; ... (*OED*, s.v.)

The *OED* recognizes both *to* infinitives and what are here termed *of-ing* complements under this sense. Illustrations include (2a) for the former and (2b) for the latter.

(2) a. I was ashamed to see it. (1885, *N.E.D.*)
    b. I began to be ashamed of sitting idle. (1752, Johnson, *Rambler*)

A separate sense 3 in the *OED* is then illustrated with *to* infinitives, but not with *of-ing* complements. The sense has two subsenses: "**a.** Reluctant through fear of shame *to*" and **b.** "With a negative: prevented or deterred by fear of shame from," and there are two examples of *to* infinitives that are later than 1700, one under each subsense:

(3) a. He would have made us ashamed to show our Heads. (1711, Addison, *Spectator*)
    b. He was not ashamed to answer that he could not live out of the royal smile. (1849, T.B. Macaulay, *Hist. Eng.*)

In broad terms, the purpose of this chapter is to approach the meanings of the patterns in (1a–b) from the point of view of Bolinger's Generalization. As noted in Chap. 1, it says that a "difference in syntactic form always spells a difference in meaning" (Bolinger 1968, 127). This Generalization is an important principle in the frameworks of cognitive grammar and of construction grammar today. In the spirit of Bolinger's Generalization, the Choice Principle, discussed in Chap. 2, is investigated in order to see whether the principle is useful in analyzing the variation between *to* infinitive and *of-ing* complements of the adjective *ashamed*, as illustrated in (1a–b).

4.2 THE CHOICE PRINCIPLE AND NON-FINITE COMPLEMENTS OF *ASHAMED*

The data for the present study come from recent American English, and two datasets are used. The first is taken from two decades of the Corpus of Historical American English, the 1940s and the 1950s. The second is from the most recent full decade of COCA, the Corpus of Contemporary American English. One-million word corpora would not be sufficient for the present project, and one reason for choosing these datasets is their size. Another reason is that data from COHA give the present study a mildly diachronic dimension. As regards the data from the most recent full decade of COCA, their inclusion is motivated by a desire to shed light on very recent usage.

Beginning with the data from COHA, the search strings used were "ashamed to [v?i*]," for the *to* infinitive, and "ashamed of [v?g*]," for the *of*-*ing* complement. These search strings retrieve 199 *to* infinitives and 38 *of*-*ing* complements, combining the 1940s and the 1950s. The total number of words in these decades of COHA is about 49 million, and the normalized frequency of *to* infinitives is therefore 4.1 per million words, and that of *of*-*ing* complements is 0.8 per million words. Neither construction is therefore extremely frequent. While the *to* infinitive is clearly the more frequent of the two, both are found with a frequency that permits comparison.

The main purpose of the present study is to investigate if the Choice Principle, introduced in Chap. 2, is a factor that has an impact on the variation between the two types of complement. It is by no means a foregone conclusion that it should have an impact, for it is recalled that in Chap. 2 it was applied to a comparison of *to* infinitive and *to*-*ing* complements. By contrast, in the present chapter the comparison concerns *to* infinitives and *of*-*ing* complements. In both cases *to* infinitives are compared with prepositional gerunds, but the prepositions are different, and it is entirely conceivable that the Choice Principle might only apply in the case of *to* infinitives and *to*-*ing* complements. On the other hand, Rudanko (2014), dealing with *to* infinitive and *of*-*ing* complements of the adjective *afraid*, provides some expectation that the principle might shed light on the comparison of *to* infinitives and *of*-*ing* complements.

There are two issues that should be dealt with as preliminaries. For the first of these, consider the sentences in (4a–b), from COHA.

(4) a. The satirical historian has not blushed to describe the naked scenes which Theodora was not ashamed to exhibit in the theatre. (1951, FIC)
b. ...one of the girls dragged me to something the other night that I was ashamed to sit through. (1954, FIC)

The sentences in (4a–b) are worth singling out because they illustrate extractions in English. As was noted in Chap. 2, extractions have a definite effect on the choice between infinitival and gerundial complement options. Extraction is relevant to the sentences in (4a–b), and in both cases the rule in question is Relativization. Because the relevance of extractions and the Extraction Principle have by now been established in work on complementation, sentences exhibiting extraction are set aside here. It may be mentioned that their total number in the two decades is relatively small, only 11, and that in accordance with the Extraction Principle, all 11 involve a *to* infinitive complement, as in (4a–b).

The second issue that should be dealt with as a preliminary concerns sentences of the type of (5a–b):

(5) a. First, I walked all the way to town because I was too ashamed to get on a streetcar. (1947, FIC)
b. He is too ashamed to call time or come out for a conference... (1955, FIC)

There is no extraction in (5a–b), but in both the adjective *ashamed* is preceded by the word *too*, and it has been noted in the literature that the *to* infinitive complement may here be linked to, and selected by, the modifier *too*, rather than by the adjective itself. Huddleston and Pullum (2002, 547) use the term "indirect complement" to refer to this type of configuration. There are five sentences with indirect complements in the dataset and it is best to omit these from a comparison of *to* infinitive and *of-ing* complements selected by the adjective itself.

When the exclusions noted in the two preliminary points are added up, they amount to 16 tokens being set aside. That is, 183 *to* infinitives and 38 *of-ing* complements remain to be examined from the point of view of the Choice Principle. To analyze the tokens in question, the same principles for separating agentive and non-agentive interpretations can be applied as in Chaps. 2 and 3.

Table 4.1 [+Choice] and [−Choice] interpretation of *to* infinitive and *of -ing* complements of *ashamed* in COHA in the 1940s and 1950s

to *inf.*		of –ing	
[+Ch]	[−Ch]	[+Ch]	[−Ch]
146	37	15	23

Table 4.1 gives information of the incidence of [+Choice] and [−Choice] readings of *to* infinitives and *of -ing* complements of *ashamed* in the present dataset.

The Chi Square is as high as 23.85, and the Choice Principle is significant at the level of <0.0001 (df = 1).

Some illustrations of both [+Choice] and [−Choice] readings of the two constructions are given in (6a–d) and (7a–d), with the (a) and (b) sentences representing *to* infinitives and the (c) and (d) sentences representing *of -ing* complements.

(6) a. We need not be ashamed to demand this act of faith on their part, ... (1945, NEWS)
   b. ... it sounds absurd, and I'm ashamed to admit it, but the kind of job I really want is to be that invaluable... (1950, MAG)
   c. ... he was young enough to feel ashamed of admitting he couldn't take it. (1940, FIC)
   d. I wasn't ashamed of working during those first eleven years I was there (1957, FIC)
(7) a. But Hayden thought, and was ashamed to be caught thinking it, that he did not desire to see Dr. Windelbank at all, nor his nimble lady. (1951, FIC)
   b. Relatives were ashamed to have an impoverished kinsman marry below his class. (1959, NF)
   c. "He was just a little ashamed of being caught talking to us!" (1940, FIC)
   d. He would bring forth evidence, said Pritt, that would make him ashamed of being English. (1959, MAG)

The lower predicates in the illustrations in (6a–d) are all [+Choice], and those in (7a–d) are all [−Choice]. For instance, regarding (6a–d), the lower predicate of (6b) is *admit it*, and an imperative of the type *Admit it!* is entirely natural. Similar considerations apply to the *of-ing* complements in (6c–d).

As for the lower predicates in (7a–d), it is observed that [–Choice] predicates can be of different types. (7a) and (7c) are similar in that the lower clauses are in the passive. This means that the understood subject in each of them corresponds to the direct object of the active version of the sentence. A direct object typically has the semantic role of Patient or Undergoer, and the subject of the passivized version has a [–Choice] interpretation, as in sentences (7a) and (7c). As for a predicate of the type *be English*, it is considered [–Choice] when used statively, as in (7d). Finally, consider the lower predicate of (7b) *have an impoverished kinsman marry below his class*. Here the verbal element that follows the NP *an impoverished kinsman* is an infinitive, instead of a past participle, as it was for instance in sentence (7c) of Chap. 3 above, but in the context of sentence (7b) here the interpretation is still that of happenstance *have*, rather than that of a causative *have*. That is, the sentence is not about relatives causing the event of an impoverished kinsman marrying beneath him, but about them potentially experiencing that event. The lower predicates of (7a–d) are therefore all [–Choice] in their contexts.

As seen in Table 4.1 the data from two decades of COHA suggests that the Choice Principle does play a role in the complement selection of the adjective *ashamed*, but it is of interest also to consider another dataset to see if it yields similar results. To shed light on current English, the years from 2000 to 2009 were chosen from COCA. The same search strings as in the case of COHA were used to collect tokens of the two patterns. The totals retrieved were 286 for the *to* infinitive and 43 for the *of-ing* complement pattern. Among them there were 20 tokens with extractions, as in (8a–b):

(8)   a. And here is something he feels strongly but is ashamed to admit. (2006, FIC)
         b. the fact that he was even with Lucy was a rule he claimed he was ashamed of breaking. (2001, FIC)

Again the extraction rule in (8a–b) is Relativization. As regards the form of the complement, the large majority of extractions, 17 of the 20, occur out of *to* infinitive complements, but it is worth mentioning that in the remaining three of them the lower clause is of the *of-ing* type, as in (8b)

The Extraction Principle is not a categorical principle, but because of its status as an established generalization affecting the complement selection properties of matrix verbs and adjectives, the 20 extractions are set aside here.

There are also 13 tokens of indirect complements, of the type identified above, where a *to* infinitive clause is linked to the modifier *too* directly preceding the adjective. Two illustrations are given in (9a–b):

(9)   a. I am too ashamed to confess that I dumped him deliberately... (2007, ACAD)
       b. Should I have gone to the elders for help instead of being too ashamed to admit what was happening in my home? (2001, FIC)

When extractions and indirect complements have been set aside, there remain 256 *to* infinitive complements and 40 *of* -*ing* complements of the adjective *ashamed* in the current dataset. Table 4.2 gives information on the incidence of [+Choice] and [−Choice] predicates among these tokens, for each year of the decade.

The figures in Table 4.2 show that *to* infinitives are clearly more frequent than *of* -*ing* complements by a clear margin for each year. They also indicate that *of* -*ing* complements are found throughout the decade, with a slight preponderance in the second half of the decade. The figures for individual

Table 4.2 [+Choice] and [−Choice] interpretations of *to* infinitive and *of* -*ing* complements of *ashamed* in COCA from 2000 to 2009

	to *inf.*		of -ing	
	[+Choice]	[−Choice]	[+Choice]	[−Choice]
2000	17	6	0	2
2001	17	6	1	4
2002	20	11	1	4
2003	24	4	0	0
2004	21	4	1	1
2005	22	10	0	1
2006	25	2	0	9
2007	14	3	2	3
2008	22	7	4	0
2009	14	7	5	2
Totals	196	60	14	26

years are too low for a comparison with respect to the Choice Principle, but the Chi square test can be applied to the totals. The Chi square is as high as 27.01 and the level of significance is <0.0001 (df = 1).

Illustrations of the [+Choice] and [−Choice] complements are given in (10a–d) and (11a–d), with the (a) and (b) sentences again representing *to* infinitives and the (c) and (d) sentences representing *of -ing* complements.

(10) a. Your once-proud newspaper should be ashamed to print such tripe. (2005, NEWS)
  b. They're so ashamed to work here that they asked us not to show their faces. (2009, SPOK)
  c. .... don't be ashamed of feeding your baby. (2007, SPOK)
  d. You're not ashamed of walking around the law firm with that pansy hairdo? (2009, FIC)

(11) a. Aria was ashamed to find herself impertinently mumbling "Thank you, m'lady." (2002, FIC)
  b. He can't manipulate silverware but is ashamed to be fed,... (2004, FIC)
  c. It makes me furious and ashamed of being an American, really, to know that this is mainly American companies (2000, SPOK)
  d. ... Class members were ashamed of their anger, ashamed of getting caught by the cops, or both. (2009, FIC)

The lower predicates in (10a–d) are all [+Choice], those in (11a–d) are all [−Choice]. The former probably do not need a comment, but as regards the latter, two of them, (11b) and (11d), are variants of passives, with the understood subjects corresponding to the direct of objects of the active versions and therefore carrying the Patient or Undergoer role. As regards the lower predicate of (11a), of the type *find oneself mumbling something*, it likewise suggests lack of volitional involvement on the part of the referent of the subject in the event, and the predicate is therefore [−Choice].

The data from COCA show that the Choice Principle continues to be a factor impacting the complement selection properties of *ashamed* even in the most recent sample of usage.

In Sect. 4.1 it was noted that the *OED* treatment of the adjective identifies two relevant senses of the adjective. The first, sense 1, might be glossed as "affected with shame" and the positive variant of the second, sense 3a, is "reluctant through fear of shame *to*." Both *to* infinitives and *of -ing* complements are featured in the *OED* under the sense of "affected with shame," but only *to* infinitives, and no *of -ing* complements, are featured under the sense of "reluctant through fear of shame *to*."

The present treatment of non-finite complements of *ashamed*, based on semantic roles and the Choice Principle, maps onto the *OED* senses of the adjective at least as far as *to* infinitives are concerned. The simple generalization is that [+Choice] readings go together with the sense of "reluctant through fear of shame *to*" and, for their part, [−Choice] readings go together with the sense of "affected with shame." For instance, (10b) might be paraphrased "they are so reluctant through shame to work here that they asked us not to show their faces." As for *of -ing* complements, the sense of "affected with shame" goes well with [−Choice] complements, as in (11c), but in the case of *of -ing* complements of the [+Choice] type it is a delicate exercise to tease apart the senses. A gloss with "reluctant through shame" seems appropriate for (10c), for instance, but in the case of the *OED* example *I began to be ashamed of sitting idle*, quoted above, it is the sense of "affected with shame" that appears to predominate.

The approach here, based on semantic roles and the Choice Principle, provides a framework for comparing *to* infinitives and *of -ing* complements as two different types of constructions. Some further remarks may be appended here on comparing *to* infinitives and *of -ing* complements when both are [−Choice].

One of the clearest types of construction involving [−Choice] complements is the type where the lower clause is in the passive, with the understood subject corresponding to the direct object of the corresponding active sentence. It is easy enough to collect additional data that are specifically targeted as these types of configurations. Here the search strings "ashamed to be [v?n*]" and "ashamed of being [v?n*]" were used, where the symbol [v?n*] stands for a past participle. For this search one decade of COCA is not sufficient, because of the specific nature of the search strings and because of the low numbers of hits, and the entire COCA was therefore used as the database. The searches retrieved 31 *to* infinitives and seven *of -ing* complements. One of the latter is adjectival, *not ashamed of being stoned* (2002, MAG), and can be set aside. Here are three examples of each type:

(12) a. Grinning, she lifted a sloppy spatula and pointed down to her big out-of-sight belly. Myra quickly waved and ducked inside, ashamed to be caught looking. (1997, FIC)

b. Bonnie had a fine figure. And she was not ashamed to be seen naked. (2003, FIC)
c. It broke my heart that he was ashamed to be seen with me. (2009, MAG)
(13) a. She offers him flowers, wordlessly, beseechingly. And he takes them, the count, now thoroughly ashamed of being caught on the verge of such a cowardly act. (1997, FIC)
b. Do you think Julian's ashamed of being raised without money,... (1993, FIC)
c. The hand was so ashamed of being tricked that it hid behind the man's back. (2005, FIC)

Infinitival *to* was placed under the Infl (corresponding to the more traditional label of Aux) in structure (1´) in Sect. 4.1, and there are scholars who have suggested that it does not carry a meaning. However, elements under Aux typically carry a meaning, and the notion of a path towards a goal seems helpful (Smith and Escobedo 2001, 552). This is the basic meaning of the preposition *to* in English. The infinitival clause is thus Goal-like in nature. In other words, the present author's position is that even though infinitival *to* is not a preposition in current English, it has its origin in the preposition *to* in earlier English, and that the original meaning of the preposition is still salient in assessing the meaning of infinitival *to* today.

As regards the preposition *of*, the *OED* makes the comment that its "primary sense" was "away," "away from" (*OED*, s.v.). Current uses may be "remote" from the primary sense (*OED*, s.v.), but the notion of separation is inherent in the primary sense of the preposition, and the semantic role of Source may be invoked to express separation. The notion of separation and the role of Source seem relevant to the interpretation of an *of-ing* complement (see also Fanego 1996, 57). The *of-ing* complement thus expresses the source or cause of the feeling of shame felt by someone.

Comparing the two constructions when both are [–Choice] is not easy, and a full account cannot be attempted here. However, it is suggested that even when the predicate in question is [–Choice], a *to* infinitive complement may still have a hint of agentivity and control. For instance in (12c), *to be seen with me* is clearly a [–Choice] predicate as a passive, but in the context of *ashamed*, there is still a hint of volition on the part of the referent of *he*. After all, it makes more sense for somebody's actions to break my heart if the other person has some degree of control over what he does. By contrast, the *of-ing* variant of the sentence—*It broke my heart that he was ashamed of being seen with me*—suggests that it broke my heart that he was affected with shame over being seen with me, or over having been seen with me, and in this case there is little or no scope for agentivity on his part regarding the event where he and I were seen together. That is, in this case my disappointment is caused by his reaction to a completed event, regardless of how the original event had come about.

Further, when *ashamed* followed by a *to* infinitive is negated, as in (12b), *And she was not ashamed to be seen naked*, there is again a suggestion of controllability, perhaps even of a stance of defiance on the part of the referent of *she*. (Such a stance of defiance, in the face of opposition or challenge, is reminiscent of the corresponding construction with the adjective *afraid*, where that adjective followed by a *to* infinitive is negated, see Rudanko 2015a, 46–47.) By contrast, it is hard to observe even the slightest touch of volitionality or agentivity in the case of the *of*-*ing* complements in (13a–c). A concomitant of this feature of the *of*-*ing* construction is that the adjective retains its sense of "affected with shame" more fully than in the case of the *to* infinitive, which may carry some tinge of volitionality. (In this connection, see Allerton's comments on the adjective *anxious* (Allerton 1988, 20).) For instance, the authentic sentence in (13b) suggests that the event denoted by the lower clause has been completed, and the question is about Julian's attitude or reaction to a completed event.[2] By contrast, when an invented *to* infinitival counterpart of sentence (13b) is constructed—*Do you think Julian's ashamed to be raised without money?*—the lower clause may suggest an ongoing process, allowing slightly more scope for volitionality on Julian's part than in the case of sentence (13b).

The framework based on the Choice Principle gives rise to one more observation. This concerns the classes of *to* infinitives that are [+Choice]. When looking through the lists of [+Choice] tokens in the second decade of COCA, the investigator cannot help noticing the high number of tokens where the main verb in the complement of *ashamed* is the verb *say*. The number of such tokens is 58. This abundance invites the investigator also to consider the complements of *say*. Such complements include NPs such as *it, this, that, anything*, but what is more noteworthy is that among the 58 tokens more than half, 30 in all, are *that* clause complements, with or without the complementizer. Here are two examples:

(14) a. I was ashamed to say that I had had those hit records (2003, SPOK)
b. ...I'm not ashamed to say the attraction is largely physical. (2006, MAG)

In (14a) the *that* clause has an overt complementizer, and in (14b) the complementizer is zero. In these sentences the highest predicate *ashamed* selects a *to* infinitive complement with the main verb *say* and *say* in turn selects a *that* clause complement. This is the syntactic structure of (14a–b), but as far as the information structure of the sentences is concerned, the middle level in the hierarchy, that is, the *say* level, does not carry much weight. The predicate *say* functions like a hinge between the top predicate *ashamed* and the *that* clause, without contributing much to the meaning of the whole. The term "hinge" comes from comments on the verb *regret* in Vosberg (2003b), where Vosberg noticed much the same phenomenon with the verb *regret*, in sentences of the type *We regret to state that there can be no longer any doubt of the plague having been introduced at Leghorn, Genoa, and Marseilles* (1826, Shelley, *The Last Man*).

Five tokens of the hinge construction are also found in the 1940s and 1950s data from COHA, amounting to a normalized frequency of 0.1 per million, but in COCA that frequency has risen to 0.15 per million. It may be added that in addition to hinge constructions with *say*, the verb *admit* also has 18 tokens of the hinge construction with *that* complements in the second decade of COCA, and that it only had three of them in the two COHA decades. The frequency of the hinge construction with *admit* has thus risen from 0.04 to 0.09 per million words. Overall, 48 of the 196 tokens of the [+Choice] type are of the hinge variety in the data from COCA, and in view of such rising frequencies it may be possible to speak of the emergence of a formulaic use of the hinge construction with *ashamed* in current American English.

4.3 Concluding Observations

This study suggests that the Choice Principle does shed light on the complement selection properties of the adjective *ashamed*. Two sets of data were considered here, the 1940s and 1950s of COHA and the second full decade of COCA, and the Principle was found to affect complement selection in both. The variation affecting non-finite complements in the case of *ashamed* concerns the alternation between *to* infinitives and *of-ing* complements. The two patterns are close to each other because both are non-finite and both involve subject control. Of the two, *to* infinitives are clearly the more frequent type of complement in both datasets, but both types were encountered in numbers that make it of interest to compare their meanings with the help of the Choice Principle. This is undertaken in the spirit of Bolinger's famous dictum that a "difference in syntactic form always spells a difference in meaning" (Bolinger 1968, 127).

The comparison revealed that no categorical rule can be given with respect to the Choice Principle. However, it was shown that *to* infinitive complements are associated with [+Choice] interpretations and that for their part *of-ing* complements are linked to [–Choice] interpretations. That is, *to* infinitives tend to have more agentive readings, while gerundive complements tend to be less agentive. This finding is in accordance with earlier work on selected verbs and adjectives, including *consent* and *accustomed*. However, in their case the variation was between *to* infinitives and *to -ing* complements, and the applicability of the Choice Principle in the study of the variation between *to* infinitives and *of-ing* complements in the case of *ashamed* naturally enhances the potential appeal of the principle, also taking into account the earlier study of *to* infinitives and *of -ing* complements of the adjective *afraid* in Rudanko (2014). Overall, the Choice Principle is of interest in that it provides a perspective on the semantic interpretations that are characteristic of the two types of non-finite complements during periods when both are selected by one and the same matrix verb or adjective.

The framework for analysis that is based on the distinction between [+Choice] and [–Choice] predicates was here also used for further discussion of the two types of non-finite complements. In the case of [–Choice] lower predicates, constructions where the lower clause embedded directly under *ashamed* is in the passive were considered, and it was suggested that while both *to* infinitives and *of -ing* complements are [–Choice] in such cases, there may still inhere a shade of agentivity to the infinitival construction, whereas with the *of-ing* pattern the adjective is more closely limited to its basic meaning of "affected with shame." In further comments on [+Choice] lower predicates selected by *ashamed*, it was noted that in the more recent dataset the hinge construction, consisting of three levels of predicates, has become prominent.

The present study invites further work on the earlier history of the adjective, and as regards [+Choice] lower predicates, it will also be of interest to see whether the hinge construction spreads further. Going beyond the adjective *ashamed*, the present study also invites further work on the Choice Principle as a factor impacting complement selection in the case of other matrix verbs and adjectives showing considerable variation between *to* infinitive and gerundial complements in recent English.

Notes

1. At a symposium on complementation in Tampere, Finland, in October 2015 Mikko Höglund presented a paper on the adjective *ashamed*, and there is some overlap between the content of that presentation and the present chapter. In spite of the overlap, it is appropriate to note that the present author drafted this chapter in this book quite independently of, and prior to, Dr. Höglund's work. Further, the focus of the present chapter is more clearly on the Choice Principle than was the case in Dr. Höglund's presentation.
2. In this connection it is also of interest to note Duffley's view that a gerund "evokes the event as a whole" (Duffley 2000, 225).

CHAPTER 5

Lexico-Grammatical Creativity in American Soap Operas: A Case Study of the Transitive *into* -*ing* Pattern

Abstract The chapter investigates the creativity of the transitive *into* -*ing* pattern in current English, with data from the Corpus of American Soap Operas. An approach to identifying creative usages is outlined, and then applied to the corpus, which comprises some 100 million words. The creative usages are then analyzed into different syntactic types, and a class of what are termed "radically creative usages" is also identified. The pattern is viewed as a type of the caused-motion construction and the semantic properties of matrix verbs selecting the pattern creatively are also examined. The chapter contains numerous illustrations of creative usages and offers a framework for their investigation.

Keywords Object control · Creative usages · Caused motion construction · Verbal subevent · Constructional subevent

5.1 Introduction

Consider sentence (1), from the Corpus of American Soap Operas, which is the default source of illustrations in this chapter:

(1) ...I pressured him into going along with me. (2009, AMC)

There are two verbs in (1), *pressure* and *go*, and in view of the evidence of Chap. 1, it can be assumed that there are two sentences in (1). The higher verb is *pressure* and it selects three arguments, the subject NP *I*, the direct object NP *him*, and the oblique complement consisting of the five overt words *into going along with me*. The semantic roles of the three arguments are Agent, Patient or Undergoer, and Goal. Given that the pattern is a control construction, the understood subject of sentence (1) is then represented by the symbol PRO, which is a pronominal NP which is phonologically zero. The pattern of sentence (1) is one of object control, since PRO is controlled by the higher object.

The pattern of sentence (1) may then be represented as in (1′):

(1′) [[I]$_{NP1}$ [pressured]$_{Verb1}$ [him]$_{NP0}$ [[into]$_{Prep}$ [[[PRO]$_{NP}$ going along with me]$_{S2}$]$_{NP}$]$_{PP}$]$_{S1}$

The structure as given in (1′) also incorporates the traditional idea that the sentential complement of *into* is a nominal clause, represented in (1′) by a sentence dominated by an NP node. The pattern of sentence (1) is a transitive pattern, and it is here termed the transitive *into -ing* pattern.

There are some patterns in English that resemble the transitive *into -ing* pattern in some ways, but should be kept separate from it. For instance, consider sentence (2):

(2) I can't rush into getting married, Craig. (2009, ATWT)

Sentence (1) undoubtedly represents a control construction with an understood subject in a sentential complement preceded by the preposition *into*. However, the matrix verb in (2) is *rush*, and this verb is used intransitively in (2). Sentence (2) is a subject control construction, since PRO is controlled by the higher subject. The intransitive pattern deserves investigation, but it is set aside in the present investigation.

In addition of the pattern of (2), consider sentence (3):

(3) I think the best thing for me is throw my energies into getting this company back on track. (2009, BB)

Sentence (3) includes the substring *throw my energies into getting this company back* and this is syntactically similar to the pattern of (1), with an NP intervening between the higher verb and the preposition *into*. However, the pattern of (3) is primarily a subject control pattern, for it is the referent of the NP *I* that is trying to get the company back on track, and the object NP, *my energies* in (3), designates a resource or an instrument at the disposal of the referent of the higher subject. The present study is limited to the object control pattern of (1), and the resource pattern of (3) is set aside here.

The transitive *into -ing* pattern has received considerable attention in the last twenty years. One strand of research has concerned the semantics of the pattern. It is generally agreed that the pattern has a telic meaning, with the action or event expressed by the lower clause involving an end point that is reached. This means that if sentence (1) as a whole is true, it follows that the proposition of the lower clause is true. That is, if it is true that I pressured him into going along with me, it follows that he did go along with me, and a sentence of the type *I pressured him into going along with me, but he did not go along with me* expresses a contradiction. This property sometimes distinguishes the present pattern from the *to* infinitive pattern. For instance, the matrix verb *pressure* also permits *to* infinitive complements involving object control, as in (4), modified from the authentic sentence in (1):

(4) I pressured him to go along with me.

However, the infinitival variant in the case of the matrix verb *pressure* is not telic, for the truth of sentence (4) does not entail the truth of the proposition of the infinitival clause. That is, a sentence of the type of *I pressured him to go along with me but he did not go along with me* does not express a contradiction. This is a noticeable difference between the two patterns in the case of matrix verbs such as *pressure*. The difference about entailment properties does not always separate the *into -ing* and *to* infinitive patterns involving object control because with some matrix predicates, the entailment property also inheres in the *to* infinitive pattern (see Rudanko 2015a, 70–71). However, the difference illustrated with *pressure* here does extend to a number of other verbs, including *cajole, coax,* and *bully*.

The entailment property of the *into -ing* pattern is related to another interesting aspect of the semantics of the pattern. This is that the pattern may be viewed as a type of the caused-motion construction with two separable subevents. As far as the present author is aware, the caused-motion analysis of the transitive *into -ing* pattern was first informally proposed in a paper given at a conference on construction grammar at Berkeley in 2000 and in print in Rudanko (2000), but a much more detailed analysis was worked out by Goldberg and Jackendoff (2004). In their article they use the term resultative in a broad sense, and it encompasses the caused-motion construction of the transitive *into -ing* pattern. They write:

> ...the meaning of a resultative sentence contains two separable subevents. One of them, the VERBAL SUBEVENT, is determined by the verb of the sentence. The other subevent, the CONSTRUCTIONAL SUBEVENT, is determined by the construction. A resultative sentence means more than just the conjunction of the verbal subevent and the constructional subevent.... That is, for the bulk of cases...the verbal subevent is the MEANS by which the constructional subevent takes place. (Goldberg and Jackendoff 2004, 538; emphasis in the original)

The verbal subevent is thus tied to the verb, *pressure* in the case of sentence (1). For its part, the constructional subevent has to do with causation, which is only to be expected since we are dealing with the caused-motion construction. To use sentence (1) as an example here, part of the meaning of the sentence might be paraphrased as follows: "I caused him to go along with me by means of pressuring him." The concept of means is clearly helpful to understanding the relation of the two subevents in sentences of the transitive *into -ing* type.

5.2 THE CREATIVITY OF THE TRANSITIVE *INTO -ING* PATTERN: A FRAMEWORK AND ILLUSTRATIONS

Another property of the transitive *into -ing* pattern that has emerged in recent work is that the pattern has been spreading in fairly recent English. Davies (2012) showed on the basis of the Corpus of Historical American English that in the early decades of the nineteenth century the construction was quite rare in American English (COHA), and Rudanko (2015b) showed on the basis of the Corpus of Late Modern English (CLMET3.0) that it was also fairly rare in British English at that time. However, from about the middle of the nineteenth century onwards the pattern has been spreading rapidly in English. As far as the twentieth century is concerned, Rudanko (2015a) investigated the *TIME* Corpus, showing that the frequency of the pattern in the 1920s was about 11 per million words, and that from the 1930s onwards it had a frequency in the region of about 20–30 tokens per million words in that corpus.

The spreading of the pattern is linked to the question of creativity and the use of the pattern with an ever larger set of matrix verbs in English. The productivity of the transitive *into -ing* pattern has been noticed and remarked on in the literature. Here is a comment from Hunston and Francis (2000), with a reference to the role of analogy:

> If we can say that someone *annoys* or *irritates* someone into doing something, then presumably we could also say that someone *angers* or *infuriates* someone into doing something. The lack of corpus evidence does not indicate that the missing occurrences are "incorrect English." If we can say that someone *relaxes* someone into doing something, can we also say that someone *calms* or *soothes* someone into doing something? This seems, intuitively, less likely, but only, perhaps, because the process of analogy has not yet progressed so far. (Hunston and Francis 2000, 102–103)

Some recent work on the transitive *into -ing* pattern has sought to shed further light on the degree of productivity of the pattern. The term "creativity" may be used here as well. The question of what counts as creative or innovative is a complex one, but one approach is to use standard works of reference as a benchmark. Two works of reference, Bridgeman et al. (1965) and Francis et al. (1996) are taken into account here. These works of reference do not use the label "transitive into *-ing* pattern," but the most common verbs selecting the pattern are listed explicitly in one or both of these works of reference. Such verbs listed include *con, deceive, fool, force, pressure*, and *talk*. (Of these *talk* has been found especially frequent with the pattern in earlier work.) However, as regards standard works of reference, the most famous is of course the *Oxford English Dictionary*, and it deserves to be taken into account. The online edition of the *OED* is the most up-to-date edition available, and for this reason it is used here. The principle is simply that if a usage with the transitive *into -ing* pattern is featured with a particular matrix verb in the *OED* or in either of the other works of reference, then it cannot be considered creative. On the other hand, if it is not featured in any one of the works of reference, then it can be considered creative.

The procedure in using the *OED* as a benchmark is clear enough in principle, but there is one detail that needs to be clarified. Unlike the more syntactic studies of Bridgeman et al. (1965) and Francis et al. (1996), the *OED* does not make a clear distinction between *into-ing* and *into* NP complements.

Quite often, verbs selecting *into* non-sentential NP complements also select *into -ing* complements and vice versa. For instance, consider the verb *fast-talk*, as in (5):

(5) You need me there to fast-talk them into admitting him under a different name. (2005, AMC)

The question is what to do in cases where a verb is featured neither in Bridgeman et al. (1965) nor in Francis et al. (1996) and the *OED* has an example of *into* NP, not of *into -ing*. The verb *fast-talk* is a case in point, for it is found in neither Bridgeman et al. (1965) nor in Francis et al. (1996), and in the *OED* there is no example of an *into -ing* complement with *fast-talk*, but there is an example of an *into* NP complement with the verb. Here is the example:

(6) Purcell and Stedman deliberately fast-talked the liquor store man into an identification (1959, C. Williams, *Man in Motion*).

The procedure adopted here is to err on the side of caution, and not to include the *into -ing* pattern as creative in such cases, provided that the semantic roles of the direct objects and those of the *into* complements are similar. For instance, if sentence (5) is compared with sentence (6), it is clear that they are similar in this case. Not including such usages is erring on the side of caution, because in this way the investigator can ensure that the role of creative usages is not exaggerated. (For an example of where the semantic roles are not similar, see Rudanko 2011, 45–46.)

The data for this study come from the Corpus of American Soap Operas. This is a corpus of approximately 100 million words, collected from a number of daytime television series, including *All My Children, As the World Turns, The Bold and the Beautiful, Days of Our Lives, General Hospital, Passions*, and *the Young and the Restless*. It is one of the Brigham Young University corpora, compiled by Mark Davies. It provides a unique insight into the language of American popular culture today. Another reason for choosing it as the database here is that it is a large database of about 100 million words, suitable for the study of less frequent constructions. (While the transitive *into -ing* pattern is frequent in Modern English, creative uses of it can be expected to be less frequent.) Further, the creative uses of the transitive *into -ing* pattern have not been investigated before in this corpus. Here the focus is on the lexico-grammatical creativity of verbs that select the pattern in the American Soap Opera Corpus. Once or twice recourse is also had to the Global Web-Based English Corpus (GloWbE), in order to shed further light on some details of the discussion.

The research task is to identify verbs that are creative, taking the benchmarks described above into account. The discussion proceeds by way of identifying different types of creativity. Syntactic considerations are taken into account when these are identified. In Sect. 5.3, comments will be appended on the semantics of the matrix verbs in creative usages in the American Soap Opera Corpus.

To collect data, the search string used was "into [v?g*]," with a verb within zero to four words to the left. (The symbol "[v?g*]" stands for the *-ing* form of a verb.) The zero in the context to the left of *into* is needed for instance for cases where the higher verb in the passive. As for the length of the context, the large majority of relevant tokens contain only one word—a pronoun or a name—between the verb and the preposition, but the search string collecting tokens where the verb is within four words to left makes provision for longer NPs. This seems adequate from the point of view of recall, given that the material is scripted conversation meant to be spoken.

Table 5.1 offers a list of matrix verbs found in the creative uses with the transitive *into -ing* pattern in the American Soap Opera Corpus, taking the bench marks described above into account, with information about the numbers of tokens.

Table 5.1 testifies to an abundance of creative usages in the American Soap Opera Corpus. Most of the verbs occur only once, but four verbs are found over ten times.

To achieve a more systematic treatment of the notion of creativity as demonstrated by matrix verbs selecting the transitive *into -ing* pattern in the corpus under review, it is possible to identify a number of different types of creativity. Consider first the sentences in (7a–c), with their matrix verbs *convince, influence,* and *possess*:

(7) a. I went down to Bermuda to try to convince Julian into taking Ethan back into the family. (2001, PASS)
   b. I just hope that Abby doesn't let anybody influence her into doing something she doesn't really want to do. (2010, YR)
   c. I don't even know what possessed me into signing those commitment papers in the first place. (2004, PASS)

Table 5.1 Creative uses of matrix verbs with the transitive *into* -*ing* pattern in the American Soap Opera Corpus

No. of tokens	Verbs
29	*strong-arm*
13	*convince*
11	*drug, scam*
7	*threaten*
6	*steamroll*
4	*snow*
3	*program, romance, spook*
2	*annoy, distract, draft, finagle, hook, pummel, snooker, squeeze, startle, sway, wish*
1	*abracadabra, arm-wrestle, assault, back, bash, bedazzle, believe, buffalo, coach, compliment, confuse, connive, corner, curse, debate, double-team, egg, extort, fake, influence, insult, jinx, lasso, leverage, possess, rattle, script, shoehorn, strangle, Svengali, tease, unnerve, use*

Neither *convince* nor *influence* nor *possess* is included among the verbs selecting the transitive *into* -*ing* pattern in Bridgeman et al. (1965) or in Francis et al. (1996). Nor are these verbs featured with *into* -*ing* complements in the treatments of these verbs in the *OED*. They therefore pass the tests for creativity described above. However, the three verbs are independently found with *to* infinitive complements in constructions with three arguments where the semantic roles of the three arguments match those found with the transitive *into* -*ing* pattern. *Convince* may be considered as a case in point, as in (8):

(8) Barril's overtures failed to convince him to come out of hiding. (*OED*, 1983, *Observer*)

The three arguments of *convince* in (7a) correspond to those in (8), and the semantic roles of the three arguments are the same. Similar considerations can be shown to hold for *influence* and *possess*. The creative aspect of the usages of (7a–c) lies in the fact that these verbs have not been documented with the *into* -*ing* complement in the three works of reference. However, since the semantic roles of (7a–c) correspond to those of (8a–c), it is possible to use the label "argument-preserving creativity" for the type of creative usage exhibited by *convince, influence* and *possess* in (7a–c).

As regards verb types, argument-preserving creativity is fairly rare among creative usages in the American Soap Opera Corpus, and seems limited to the three verbs discussed and illustrated. At the same time, the one verb *convince* is the second most frequent of all the verbs identified (after *strong-arm*), with 13 tokens.

A far more frequent type of creativity, in terms of verb types, is illustrated by the usages in (9a–h), with the matrix verbs, *bedazzle, drug*, etc., presented in alphabetical order:

(9) a. ... she bedazzled a judge into taking my rights away as a parent. (2004, PASS)
 b. ... she tried to drug a guy into marrying her. (2007, AMC)
 c. ... Roxy hasn't spoken to her since she jinxed her into losing all of her money at the tables in A.C. (2008, OLTL)
 d. I've got bigger battles than trying to pummel you into being my friend. (2010, AMC)
 e. She snowed the entire town, practically the entire country into believing she was a therapist. (2002, OLTL)
 f. And if I say no, what are you going to do—strangle me into doing it? (2005, AMC)
 g. You strong-armed the union head into dropping his demands and settling. (2010, AMC)
 h. You want me to threaten him into liking me again? (2009, GH)

The matrix verbs in (9a–h) illustrate verbs that commonly select two arguments. For instance we might consider the first two, *bedazzle* and *drug*, as in these examples from the corpus being investigated here:

(10) a. I guess you're not the only one bewitched and bedazzled by the beautiful Theresa. (2004, PASS)
 b. You must have drugged me. (2004, AMC)

In the *Shorter OED* the sense of *bedazzle* is given as "to dazzle completely or thoroughly, confuse by excess of brilliance," that of *drug* is given as "to administer a drug to (a person etc.), esp. in order to stupefy or poison." These senses occur naturally in sentences where the verbs select two arguments, as in (10a–b). However, in the examples of the transitive *into -ing* pattern in (9a–h) each of the verbs selects three arguments. When the sentences are viewed as representing a type of the caused-motion construction, it is possible to say that there are again two subevents involved, the verbal and the constructional, and that the third argument found in the tokens is supplied by the construction. The type of creativity may therefore be labeled "argument-augmenting creativity." In the case of the matrix verbs of (9a–h) the construction augments the argument structure of the matrix verb by one argument.

Support for the constructional analysis of the sentences of (9a–h) comes from the semantic interpretation of these sentences. The sentences do not simply mean that two subevents took place, but that the verbal subevent expresses the means by which the constructional subevent took place, in accordance with the generalization formulated by Goldberg and Jackendoff (2004). To consider sentence (9a) as an example, part of its meaning is along the lines "she caused a judge to take my rights away as a parent by means of dazzling him/her completely." Analogous glosses are relevant to the other sentences in (9a–h).

Most of the verbs used creatively in the American Soap Opera Corpus are of the argument-augmenting type. More specifically, they are of the type of the matrix verbs in (9a–h), that is, the one-argument-augmentation type, where one additional argument is supplied by the construction. Such additional verbs include *arm-wrestle, assault, buffalo, confuse, corner, curse, distract, double-team, drug, finagle, hook, lasso, pummel, rattle, scam, snooker, squeeze, startle, steamroll, sway, tease, unnerve,* and *wish*. Even the verb *script* appears to be of the same type. It is found in the following example:

(11) So your daddy and your uncle Bo could script you into bringing me down...(2007, DAYS)

The verb *script* has the basic sense of "adapt (a story, novel, etc.) for broadcasting or filming" (*Shorter OED*, part of the definition of the sense of the verb *script*). The nature of the direct object in (11) is rather different from what it is in the definition of the sense since it is [+Human] in (11), but the notion of adapting seems akin to the notion of influencing, and on this basis the usage can be accommodated here. Part of the meaning of sentence (11) might be expressed along the lines of "your uncle Bo could cause you to bring me down by means of scripting (adapting) you."

A note may also be appended on *arm-wrestle* and *double-team*. Consider (12a–b):

(12) a. I'm so sick of Ryan and everyone else trying to arm-wrestle me into making a decision. (2006, AMC)
b. And I only said I'd try because you and Captain Control double-teamed me into saying yes. (2006, BB)

As regards *arm-wrestle*, the OED mostly points to intransitive uses of the verb, but the verb can also be used transitively, at least in recent English, as in this example from GloWbE:

(13) ...the sheer joy of it all when she accepts the challenge to arm wrestle Edward's big brother, Emmett... (GloWbE, US).

The verb can therefore be accommodated in the set of the one-argument-augmentation type verbs.

As for *double-team*, consider sentence (14):

(14) ...Kansas City regularly double teamed Gates and bracketed him in scoring position (GloWbE, US)

In (14) *double-team* selects an object NP as its complement, and such sentences support the inclusion of the verb among verbs of the one-argument-augmentation type.

The verb *double-team* also brings up an interesting limitation of the creativity of the transitive *into* -*ing* pattern. The OED entry of the verb features *on* NP complements of the verb, as for instance in (15):

(15) On the next day we double-teamed on one section of his army. (1904, T. Watson, *Bethany*)

One or two *on* NP complements are found with the verb in GloWbE as well, alongside NP complements, which are more numerous. The interesting point is then that an *into* -*ing* complement is quite unidiomatic when the entity being influenced is represented with *on* NP, as in this invented sentence, modeled on (12b): *They double-teamed on me into saying yes.*

Returning to the positive evidence of the American Corpus of Soap Operas, the predominance of matrix verbs of the type where the construction supplies one additional argument raises the question of whether there are creative usages where two additional arguments are supplied by the construction. It has been suggested in earlier work that as far as non-creative usages are concerned, the verb *talk* shows this kind of behavior. An NP complement is certainly possible with *talk*, as in *talk politics*, but the semantic role of the object NP differs from the role that it has when the verb occurs with the transitive *into -ing* pattern, as in *talk someone into doing something*, and it is therefore reasonable to think of the construction supplying two arguments in this case (Rudanko 2011, 20–21).

Augmentation by two arguments also appears to be found in the case of creative usages. Consider the verbs *connive* and *debate*, as illustrated in (16a–b).

(16) a. ... she's connived Ethan into working with the police in trying to track down you and the baby. (2005, PASS)
 b. You're not gonna debate me into changing how I feel. (2003, YR)

The verb *connive*, with the sense "to turn a blind eye to (an action one ought to oppose, but which one secretly sympathizes with)" (*Shorter OED*, part of the definition of sense 3), commonly selects an *at* NP complement, as in *Officials connive at prohibited kindness*, GloWbE, US, *bostonreview.net*). However, the notion of influencing seems relevant to (16a), but does not seem salient in the example of an *at* NP complement, and therefore it is suggested here that in the case of *connive* the construction supplies the matrix verb with two additional arguments.

As for *debate*, it can select NP complements easily enough as in *They get panels of "experts" to debate a newsclip, which itself is frequently abridged.* (GloWbE, US, blogspot.suntimes.com). However, again the notion of influencing is hardly salient to the interpretation of the direct object in the case of an NP complement, and it seems appropriate again, as in the case of *talk*, to say that the construction supplies two arguments in (16b).

While matrix verbs that involve the construction supplying two additional arguments are found in the corpus under review, creative usages involving such verbs appear to be rather rare. It is also worth noting that both *connive* and *debate* only occur once in the corpus with the transitive *into* -*ing* pattern.

The types of argument-preserving and argument-augmenting creativity do not exhaust the types of creativity involving the transitive *into* -*ing* pattern in the American Soap Opera Corpus. In Rudanko (2015a, 83–84) a more radical criterion of creativity was introduced. According to this approach, a usage is creative only if these conditions are satisfied: the verb is not found in the relevant lists of matrix verbs selecting *into* -*ing* complements in Bridgeman et al. (1965) nor in Francis et al. (1996) AND the verb in question is not included as a verb in the *OED*. When the verb is not featured in earlier work, the question of augmenting its argument structure, as it occurs in an earlier work of reference, does not arise in the first place.

Consider the following examples of the transitive *into* -*ing* pattern from the American Corpus of Soap Operas:

(17) a. ...David Blaine couldn't abracadabra J.R. into playing nice. (2005, AMC)
 b. I wasn't able to Svengali Lulu into falling for Logan. (2007, GH)

The two verbs *abracadabra* and *Svengali* demonstrate what may be termed the "radically creative type." In their case, the verbs are not in the lists in Bridgeman et al. (1965) nor in Francis et al. (1996) and the *OED* does not recognize the uses of the two words as verbs. For the word *abracadabra* the *OED* has an entry for a noun—with two senses, one of them with two subsenses—and for an interjection. When used as an interjection it is an "exclamation imparting supposed magical powers" (*OED*, s.v.), and one of the senses of the noun is given as "Something supposedly endowed with special power or efficacy; magic; (also) rigmarole, hocus-pocus" (*OED*, s.v. sense 2). Such senses of the noun and of the interjection are clearly related to the meaning of the word when used as a verb selecting the transitive *into* -*ing* pattern, but because the word is not featured as a verb in the *OED* at all, the usage is viewed as a type of radical creativity.

With such creative coinages that are not established words in the language, there is a strong case for regarding the transitive *into* -*ing* pattern as a type of the caused-motion construction. The reason is that a caused-motion interpretation, with the constructional and verbal subevents separated and related to each other on the basis of the notion of means as described, yields a suitable paraphrase for interpreting the sentence. Thus sentence (17a), for instance, may be glossed along the lines "David Blaine could not cause J.R. to play nice by means of (uttering) a magical word."

The verb *Svengali*, as used in sentence (17b), is another example of radical creativity. The *OED* has an entry for the word, but as a noun, not as a verb. The noun designates a character — a "musician and hypnotist" — in a novel by George Du Maurier, and in a transferred sense a "person who exercises a controlling or mesmeric influence on another, freq. for some sinister purpose" (*OED*). The sense of the verb *Svengali* is related to the sense of the noun in the *OED* entry, and part of the meaning of sentence (17b) is along the lines of "I was not able to cause Lulu to fall for Logan by means of exerting a mesmeric influence on her."

5.3 On the Semantics of Creative Uses of the Transitive *into -ing* Pattern

It is also appropriate to inquire whether generalizations can be identified regarding the semantics of creative usages. In particular, it is worth considering whether the matrix verbs in question are of a certain semantic type. In general terms, the verbs in question, when used with the transitive *into -ing* pattern express the notion of influencing: the referent of the higher subject influences the referent of the object in some way. This is in accordance with a well-established generalization about the meaning conveyed by object-control patterns (see Sag and Pollard 1991, 66). However, it is possible to inquire further into the nature of influencing that is salient in the case of creative usages. In constructional terms, the task is to formulate generalizations about the types of subevents that are found in creative usages. The underlying assumption here is that the verbs selecting a certain pattern of complementation do not exhibit random variation in their meanings. Instead, they tend to be linked to certain types of meanings. While no one-to-one mappings can be maintained, the number of different semantic types tends to be fairly low for different syntactic patterns.

When considering the semantics of creatively used verbs, it is appropriate to proceed from earlier work on the pattern even where such earlier work was not focused on creative usages. The point of interest is whether matrix verbs in creative usages can be accommodated in semantic classes that are similar to those set up for verbs selecting the transitive *into -ing* pattern in general. Given the role of analogy referred to above, similar semantic classes can be expected to emerge, but it is still worth finding out whether this is the case.

Taking advantage of the framework, outlined above, of the two subevents involved in the semantic interpretation of the pattern, the constructional and the verbal, it is possible to use the meaning of the constructional subevent as the overall characterization of the meaning of the pattern and then to identify semantic classes of verbs on the basis of the nature of the means employed to bring about the constructional subevent. To facilitate discussion, it is helpful to make use of the labels introduced in the syntactic bracketing of (1′): the symbol NP_1 stands for the subject of the matrix verb, or its referent, the symbol NP_0 stands for the object of the matrix verb, or its referent, and the symbol S_2 stands for the lower clause or the state of affairs or action designated by the lower clause.

Table 5.2 offers a framework for the semantic analysis of creative matrix verbs.

The semantic classes in Table 5.2 do not imply that the verbs of any one class are synonymous with each other. The classes are only intended to

Table 5.2 Semantic classes of creatively used matrix verbs with the transitive *into -ing* pattern

NP_1 causes NP_0 to perform or to bring about S_2
by means of deception or trickery
abracadabra, bedazzle, confuse, connive, distract, drug, fake, finagle, jinx, possess, scam, snooker, snow, Svengali
by means of exerting force or pressure
arm-wrestle, assault, back, bash, buffalo, corner, double-team, draft, extort, hook, lasso, leverage, pummel, shoehorn, squeeze, strangle, steamroll, strong-arm
by means of arousing fear, irritation, anger, annoyance, confusion, surprise
annoy, curse, insult, rattle, spook, startle, tease, threaten, unnerve
by means of enticing, flattery or persuasion
compliment, convince, debate, egg, romance
by other specific means
believe, coach, program, script, use, wish
by nonspecific means
influence, sway

capture shared ingredients of meaning among sets of verbs when they select the transitive *into -ing* pattern. It is also in the nature of such classifications that some verbs are easier to accommodate in semantic classes than others and there may sometimes be a gray area between the classes. For instance, one might class *threaten* with verbs of pressure, but because the verb suggests arousing fear, it is classed among the verbs featuring an emotion. At the same time, for most verbs the decision can be made with a fair degree of confidence.

With such caveats taken for granted, Table 5.2 still suggests that the majority of matrix verbs cluster around verbs expressing exerting force or pressure, on the one hand, and those expressing deception or trickery, on the other. This is certainly true as regards the numbers of individual verb types in the semantic classes, and it is also true as regards the tokens of the verb types in the corpus. There are some matrix verbs, including c*onvince* and perhaps *threaten*, from outside of these two semantic classes that are used frequently in the corpus, but most verbs that are found more than once are from the two semantic classes. Verbs with only one token in the corpus also cluster around these two classes. The class of verbs featuring emotion is also relatively large, especially if *threaten* is included in it. *Convince* is a high-frequency verb of the fourth class.

Several of the verbs expressing force or pressure have basic or literal senses, including *arm-wrestle, corner, pummel, squeeze*, to name a few, that convey the use of force. When used with the *into -ing* pattern, the meaning of the verb is typically more figurative or metaphorical. Consider the illustrations in (18a–d):

(18)   a. My sister just—just said that Josh cornered her into having sex, and you are defending that slime? (2006, AMC)
        b. ...and Kay to be the rest of the wedding party and lassoed Noah Bennett into playing the part of the priest. (2004, PASS)
        c. And with Luis ready to pummel our imposter into telling the truth, our role in this charade could be exposed at any moment...(2001, PASS)
        d. Your pitiful attempt to strong-arm me into signing this agreement proves that you're bluffing. (2001, YR)

For instance, *lasso* has the basic meaning of "catch (as) with a lasso" (*Shorter OED*) and *pummel* has the basic meaning of "beat or strike repeatedly, esp. with the fists; pound, thump" (*Shorter OED)*. As used with the transitive *into* -*ing* pattern, the verbs take on a meaning that is certainly related to the basic meaning, but the concrete meaning is normally not literally applicable. For instance, part of the meaning of sentence (18b) might be glossed "[someone] caused Noah Bennett to play the part of a priest, as if by means of by catching him with a lasso," and part of the meaning of sentence (18c) might be glossed "Luis ready to cause the imposter to tell the truth as if by means of beating the imposter."

There are also some verbs that express a type of influencing that is different from the concepts that are relevant to the first four classes. *Coach* may be illustrated here. The example is given in (19):

(19) I kinda coached J.J. into making a good apology. (2007, ATWT)

The example with *coach* is of interest because the transitive *into* -*ing* pattern has been linked to a negative prosody in the literature (Wulff et al. 2007, 274–275). Many of the tokens given above are in accordance with this expectation, but sentence (19) is among those that are not negative, perhaps indicating that the pattern is spreading further.

5.4 Concluding Observations

The present study offers further evidence of the creative potential of the transitive *into* -*ing* pattern. Strict limits were placed on what is considered creative here, and most uses of the pattern in the American Soap Opera Corpus are therefore set aside in this study.

While this study therefore does not examine the overall incidence of the pattern, it brings to light creative usages of different types. Perhaps most creative are those tokens where the pattern is selected by a matrix verb that is not recognized as a verb in the *OED* at all. The number of such examples, termed radically creative here, is not large, but given the comprehensiveness of the *OED* and the fact that TV drama represents scripted speech, it is remarkable that two were found.

Apart from radically creative tokens, the discussion of creativity proceeded on the basis of the argument structures of the matrix verbs selecting the transitive *into* -*ing* pattern. From this perspective, creative usages involving argument structure preserving matrix verbs selecting the pattern included *convince*, but their overall number is not very large. By far the largest number of creative usages involves argument augmentation. More particularly, most of the matrix verbs in question were one-argument-augmentation verbs. For instance, a verb such as *strangle* ordinarily selects two arguments, a subject argument and an object argument, but the creative usage with an *into -ing* complement involves the addition of a third argument. A constructional approach, with a constructional and a verbal subevent and a specific relation between them, was seen to be helpful in shedding light on the semantics of the resulting pattern.

As regards the senses of matrix verbs selecting the pattern in creative usages, it was found that most of them can be grouped into a fairly small set of classes. The classes of verbs of deception and of those expressing force or pressure were the most prominent among them.

The present study invites further work on the creative potential of the transitive *into -ing* pattern. There seems little doubt in view of the abundance of the creative usages pointed out in Rudanko (2005, 2015a) and in this study that if and when further, and even larger corpora are investigated, further creative uses of the pattern will be discovered. One perspective that deserves investigation in this context concerns creative usages in other text types, and the question of whether some text types may be more creative than others. A fairly large number of creative usages were identified in the American Soap Opera Corpus, and it will be of interest to investigate whether this is a text type that especially favors them. A meaning ingredient typical of the transitive *into -ing* pattern is that of influencing, and they are also often used in reporting acts of influencing. One may speculate that soap operas with their human interest stories may often involve influencing and reports of influencing, providing a fertile ground for creativity as far as the transitive *into -ing* pattern is concerned. Whether this speculation is correct can only be decided in a broader study of different text types, and it will also be desirable in that context to pay attention to other object-control patterns and the question of creativity in their case.

Some of the creative usages identified in this study and in subsequent work may also deserve the status of being recorded in major works of reference, especially the *OED*, given its aim of comprehensive coverage. Four verbs were identified here that were used more than ten times in the corpus in a creative way, and a further six were used more than twice. While it is not even reasonable to expect that lexicographers would include every creative usage in a dictionary, the frequency of occurrence does matter, and the matrix verbs that are found with the pattern with a fair degree of frequency may be considered for inclusion. As to where the cut-off point should be is a question that the present author is happy to leave to those editing large dictionaries.

It may be hoped that later work may benefit from the approach to analyzing different types of creativity outlined here. It may also be possible to apply the framework, making use of radical creativity and various types of argument augmentation, to other types of lexico-grammatical creativity within the system of English predicate complementation.

CHAPTER 6

Concluding Observations

Abstract The chapter reviews the main findings of the volume. In Chaps. 2 through 4 the approach is head based in that the argument structure of a particular verb or adjective that selects both *to* infinitive and gerundial complements is considered in order to gain new information on how to explain the variation between the two types of non-finite complements. The present author believes that the Choice Principle can contribute to this research task in the case of each of the matrix predicates considered, and the empirical findings in support of this hypothesis are summed up in this chapter. For its part, Chap. 5 examines a particular gerundial pattern, the transitive *into -ing* pattern, suggesting that the pattern is productive in current English. The task is then to provide a framework for the analysis of innovative usages and the main features of the framework proposed are summarized in this chapter.

Keywords Complementation · Complement taking predicate · Subject control · Object control · Understood subject

The system of English predicate complementation offers a fascinating subject for investigation because of its complexity. The present book has the purpose of shedding light on *to* infinitive and gerundial complements, with a focus on variation and change in recent English and on the semantic properties of these two types of sentential complements. The method adopted in Chaps. 2 through 4 consisted in selecting a matrix verb or adjective that selects, or has selected, both types of sentential complement in recent English, and these case studies were then used to shed light on the properties of the complements. Chap. 5 adopted a slightly different perspective in proceeding from one particular gerundial pattern and then in inquiring into types of innovative usages of that pattern selected by different matrix verbs.

Chapter 2 investigates *to* infinitive and *to -ing* complements of the matrix verb *consent*. Descriptively, it is observed that the adjective has become relatively rare in current English, but that when the British English and American English segments of the GloWbE Corpus are examined, over 200 *to* infinitive complements are found. The totals of *to -ing* complements are lower than a hundred for each of the two regional varieties, but they are still sizeable enough to be of interest, and the relative proportions of *to -ing* complements are considerably higher compared to *to* infinitives than in older decades of COHA. The two datasets therefore show evidence of considerable variation between the two patterns in current English.

The variation between the two non-finite types of complement led in Chap. 2 to an inquiry into the factors that may impact the variation in question. The Extraction Principle is by now a well-established generalization bearing on the choice between the two types of complement and it was considered first. As far as the present data were concerned, the numbers of extractions were relatively low, which restricts the usefulness of the principle in this case. Still, as far as the extractions that did occur were concerned, they were found to be as predicted by the principle.

The other principle investigated was the Choice Principle. It is based on the nature of the lower predicate and the semantic role of the understood subject of the complement clause selected by the matrix verb. The principle predicts that *to* infinitive complements tend to be found with agentive lower subjects (and predicates), designated as [+Choice], and that *to -ing* complements tend to go together with non-agentive lower subjects (and predicates), designated as [−Choice]. No categorical rule can be given, but the tendencies were observed to be statistically significant both in the American and British English datasets.

Chapter 3 turned to *to* infinitive and *to -ing* complements of the adjective *subject*. It was observed, on the basis of major dictionaries, that the adjective has senses of the type "to be affected" and "under obligation . . . to do something." Such senses are very compatible with [−Choice] interpretations of lower predicates, and the recent history of the complements of the adjective is therefore of interest from the point of view of the Choice Principle. A decade-by-decade survey of COHA revealed that *to* infinitives clearly predominated over *to* -*ing* complements with the adjective in the nineteenth century, but that in the twentieth century *to* -*ing* complements became considerably more frequent than *to* infinitives. The Choice Principle offers a perspective to understand the change, in the context of the Great Complement Shift.

While the change affecting non-finite complements of the adjective *subject* is clear enough, the data from COHA also showed that in the nineteenth century, and especially in the 1840s, the adjective was commonly found with *to* infinitives even in contexts where the lower clause was clearly and even prototypically [−Choice], with passive lower clauses being frequent examples. This finding is of theoretical interest from the point of view of the grammatical analysis of infinitival *to* in relatively recent English. The analysis adopted and used in this volume is based on the view that in current English infinitival *to* should be accommodated under the Aux node and that the "drift of the English infinitive from a nominal to a verbal character" is "now virtually complete" (Denison 1998, 266). A major argument, perhaps the clearest argument (see Warner 1993, 64), underlying this view is that in current English infinitival *to* permits VP Deletion, whereas prepositional *to* does not. However, as has been observed by Denison, VP Deletion constructions with infinitival *to* were rare until the middle of the nineteenth century, and it was from that time onwards that they become increasingly frequent (Denison 1998, 201). A small-scale case study was undertaken here of the matrix verb *want* from the perspective of VP Deletion, and the results confirmed Denison's point. In view of these considerations it was suggested in Chap. 3 that the "drift of the English infinitive from a nominal to a verbal character" was at a noticeably less advanced stage in the first half of the nineteenth century, and therefore *to* infinitives were not at all incompatible with [−Choice] interpretations at that time. The ease with which the adjective *subject* selected *to* infinitives that were [−Choice] in the nineteenth century, especially before the middle of the century, may thus shed some additional light on the grammatical status of *to* infinitives. In this respect the present study of the adjective *subject* invites additional work on the history and grammatical status of infinitival *to* in the nineteenth century, including a more comprehensive study of the history of VP Deletion in the nineteenth century.

At the same time, Chap. 3 also revealed that while there has been a change favoring *to* -*ing* complements over *to* infinitives in non-finite complements of the adjective *subject* in recent English, some residues of *to* infinitives can still be found, even in current English. Such usages were linked to conservative text types in Chap. 3.

Chapter 4 also had a focus on the Choice Principle. It was observed that in recent English the adjective *ashamed* selects both *to* infinitives and prepositional gerunds introduced by the preposition *of*, with the gerundial pattern being termed the *of -ing* pattern. It was suggested that the two patterns are similar enough in their meanings to warrant comparison. The data examined came from two decades of COHA, the 1940s and 1950s, and from the years from 2000 to 2009 of COCA. *To* infinitives were found to be more frequent in each part of the data examined, but *of -ing* complements were also frequent enough to make comparison possible. A major objective of the investigation was to find out if the Choice Principle might shed light on the variation between the two types of non-finite complements. The principle was found to be a salient factor, with *to* infinitives tending to involve a [+Choice] interpretation of the sentential complement and *of -ing* complements tending to involve a [−Choice] interpretation of the complement.

While the Choice Principle was found to be a significant factor impacting the variation between *to* infinitive and *of -ing* complements of the adjective *ashamed*, it bears emphasizing that it is only a tendency, not a rigid rule. From this perspective it is important not only to pay attention to significant tendencies but also to usages that run counter to the tendencies. In Chap. 4 the entire COCA was then examined with respect to constructions where *ashamed* is followed by a passive infinitive or a passive gerund. This context is an environment par excellence for a complement with a [−Choice] interpretation, and in spite of the salience of the Choice Principle to non-finite complements of *ashamed*, it was observed that fairly large numbers of *to* infinitives were encountered with [−Choice] interpretations. This made it possible to probe further into their interpretation. Judgments can be delicate in such cases, but it was suggested that even where the lower clause is [−Choice], the use of the *to* infinitive variant may still express a hint of controllability and agentivity. Here it is possible to consider the authentic sentence *It broke my heart that he was ashamed to be seen with me* (COCA 2009, MAG), where the lower predicate is [−Choice], but where the *to* infinitive still suggests some element of controllability on the part of the referent of *he*. This may be compared with *It broke my heart that he was ashamed of being seen with me*, which suggests less control and less agentivity on the part of the referent of *he* and a more literal interpretation of the meaning of *ashamed* ("affected with shame").

In this connection it is also worth noting separately the construction where the adjective *ashamed* followed by a *to* infinitive is negated, as for instance in *And she was not ashamed to be seen naked* (COCA 2003 FIC). The lower predicate is again [−Choice], since the (understood) subject of the passive corresponds to the direct object of the active, but in spite of this, there is again a suggestion of controllability and agentivity in the interpretation of the sentence. In the sentence the *to* infinitive may in fact convey a stance of defiance, in the face of challenge or opposition, on the part of the referent of the understood subject. This is reminiscent of what was observed with the adjective *afraid* in Rudanko (2015a, 47). In the case of the gerundial complement the focus is more on the literal meaning of *ashamed*. From this perspective, the present investigation thus seeks to shed light on the semantic difference between the two constructions, in the spirit of Bolinger's Principle.

In Chap. 5 a pattern-based approach was adopted to investigate innovative or creative usages of one particular gerundial pattern, the transitive *into -ing* pattern. After a brief comparison of this pattern with the corresponding *to* infinitive pattern, the discussion turned to identifying usages that are creative in terms of the argument structure of the relevant matrix verb. The notion of creativity is not easy to pin down, but one way to approach the issue is to consider major works of reference. In this study Bridgeman et al. (1965) and Francis et al. (1996) and the *OED* were taken into account, and usages were not included as creative where these are already featured in at least one of these standard works of reference with a particular matrix verb. The corpus considered here was the Corpus of American Soap Operas, to give information on the use of the transitive *into -ing* pattern in scripted conversation in very recent American English.

Identifying and illustrating creative uses of the transitive *into -ing* pattern was one concern in the chapter, but another objective was to outline a framework for the analysis of the different types of matrix verbs that select the pattern creatively in the corpus. Underlying the analysis was the view that the transitive *into -ing* pattern represents a type of the caused-motion construction, with two separable subevents, where the verbal subevent typically expresses the means by which the constructional subevent takes place. From a syntactic perspective, most verbs turned out to be of the argument-augmenting type, where their use with the transitive *into -ing* pattern involves augmenting the argument structure of the verb with one additional argument, or sometimes even with two arguments. These types involving argument augmentation are based on relating the uses of the matrix verbs with the transitive *into -ing* pattern to uses of the verbs that occur independently, with meanings that can be related to the meanings of the verbs when they select the transitive *into -ing* pattern.

In addition, a separate type was set up for those matrix verbs that are not included as verbs at all in any of the three standard works of reference, not even in the *OED*. The number of such radically creative matrix verbs was not high, but *abracadabra,* used as a matrix verb, was a case in point. As regards the semantics of usages with radically creative matrix verbs, it is suggested that these usages can be understood on the basis of the assumption of two subevents that is a feature of the analysis of the caused-motion construction.

The present volume invites further work, for instance on factors influencing variation and change in the system of English predicate complementation, taking the Great Complement Shift into account. Several chapters of the present volume suggest, in the view of the present author, that case studies of individual verbs, adjectives, and nouns can lead to a better understanding of such factors. The large electronic corpora compiled and made available to the scholarly community by Mark Davies provided the indispensable foundation for all the proposals and hypotheses in this volume. Among the proposals the Choice Principle is prominent, and it is put forward as a principle that may bear on variation between *to* infinitives and gerundial complements when both options are available in principle to a matrix verb, adjective or noun. Whether the Choice Principle will obtain the status of the Extraction Principle is for later work to determine. The Choice Principle, of course, only represents a tendency, not a hard and fast categorical rule, and it is also of great interest to investigate authentic tokens that run counter to it, for such tokens may shed light on the semantic properties of the construction in question, as was suggested in the discussion of the adjective *ashamed* in Chap. 4.

The present author began his work on the system of English predicate complementation with some articles in the journal *English Studies* more than three decades ago. Whether the present volume is his last publication in this area (or in any area) remains to be seen, but it has certainly been a pleasure to have worked with others in this fascinating area of English linguistics over the years.

REFERENCES

Allerton, David. 1988. "Infinitivitis" in English. In *Essays on the English Language and Applied Linguistics on the Occasion of Gerhard Nickel's 60th Birthday*, eds. J. Klegraf and D. Nehls, 11–23. Heidelberg: Julius Groos.

Ball, C.N. 1994. Automated Text Analysis: Cautionary Tales. *Literary and Linguistic Computing* 9: 294–303.

Berman, Arlene. 1970. Agent, Experiencer, and Controllability. In *Mathematical Linguistics and Automatic Translation*, Report NSF-24, ed. S. Kuno, 203–237. Cambridge, MA: Harvard University.

Bolinger, Dwight. 1968. Entailment and the Meaning of Structures. *Glossa* 2: 119–127.

Brezina, Vaclav and Miriam Meyerhoff. 2014. Significant or Random? A Critical Review of Sociolinguistic Generalizations Based on Large Corpora. *International Journal of Corpus Linguistics* 19: 1–28.

Bridgeman, Lorraine, Dale Dillinger, Constance Higgins, P. David Seaman, and Floyd A. Shank. 1965. *More Classes of Verbs in English*. Bloomington, IN: Indiana University Linguistics Club.

Chomsky, Noam. 1981. *Lectures on Government and Binding*. Dordrecht: Foris.

Chomsky, Noam. 1986. *Knowledge of Language. Its Nature, Origin and Use*. New York: Praeger.

Collins Cobuild Dictionary = *Collins Cobuild Advanced Learner's English Dictionary*. 2003. 4th edn. Glasgow: HarperCollins.

Davies, Mark. 2012. Some Methodological Issues Related to Corpus-Based Investigations of Recent Syntactic Changes in English. In *The Oxford Handbook of the History of English*, eds. Terttu Nevalainen and Elizabeth Traugott, 157–174. Oxford: Oxford University Press.

Davies, William and Stanley Dubinsky. 2004. *The Grammar of Raising and Control.* Malden, MA: Blackwell.

De Smet, Hendrik. 2013. *Spreading Patterns. Diffusional Change in the English System of Complementation.* Oxford: Oxford University Press.

Denison, David. 1998. Syntax. In *The Cambridge History of the English Language, Volume 4 1776–1997*, ed. S. Romaine. Cambridge: Cambridge University Press.

Dowty, David. 1991. Thematic Proto-Roles and Argument Selection. *Language* 67: 547–619.

Duffley, Patrick. 2000. Gerund Versus Infinitive as Complement of Transitive Verbs in English: The Problems of "Tense" and "Control." *Journal of English Linguistics* 28: 221–248.

Fanego, Teresa. 1996. The Development of Gerunds as Objects of Subject-Control Verbs in English (1400–1760). *Diachronica* 13: 29–62.

Francis, Gill, Susan Hunston, and Elizabeth Manning (eds). 1996. *Collins Cobuild Grammar Patterns 1: Verbs.* London: HarperCollins.

Goldberg, Adele and Ray Jackendoff. 2004. The English Resultative as a Family of Constructions. *Language* 80: 532–568.

Herbst, Thomas, David Heath, Ian Roe, and Dieter Götz. 2004. *A Valency Dictionary of English.* Berlin: Mouton de Gruyter.

Huddleston, Rodney and Geoffrey K. Pullum. 2002. *The Cambridge Grammar of the English Language.* Cambridge: Cambridge University Press.

Hundt, Marianne. 2004. Animacy, Agentivity, and the Spread of the Progressive in Modern English. *English Language and Linguistics* 8: 47–69.

Hunston, Susan and Gill Francis. 2000. *Pattern Grammar: A Corpus-Driven Approach to the Lexical Grammar of English.* Amsterdam: John Benjamins.

Jackendoff, Ray. 1990. *Semantic Structures.* Cambridge, MA: MIT Press.

Jespersen, Otto. 1940. *A Modern English Grammar on Historical Principles. Part V Syntax.* Volume IV. Reprinted 1961. London and Copenhagen: George Allen and Unwin/Ejnar Munksgaard.

Kuno, Susumu. 1970. Some Properties of Referential Noun Phrases. In *Studies in General and Oriental Linguistics Presented to Shiro Hattori on the Occasion of His Sixtieth Birthday*, eds. Roman Jakobson and Shigeo Kawamato, 348–373. Tokyo: TEC.

Leech, Geoffrey, Marianne Hundt, Christian Mair, and Nicholas Smith. 2009. *Change in Contemporary English.* Cambridge: Cambridge University Press.

Mair, Christian. 1990. *Infinitival Complement Clauses in English.* Cambridge: Cambridge University Press.

Mukherjee, Joybrato. 2015. Responses to Davies and Fuchs. *English World-Wide* 31(1): 34–37.

Noonan, Michael. 1985. Complementation. In *Language Typology and Syntactic Description*. Volume II. Complex Constructions, ed. Timothy Shopin. Cambridge: Cambridge University Press.

OALD = *Oxford Advanced Learner's Dictionary of Current English*, ed. by A. S. Hornby. 1979. 3rd edn. (2005. 7th edn.). Oxford: Oxford University Press.

OED = *The OED Online (OED Online)*. 2008. Includes the full text of the 2nd edition (1989) and the 3 Additions. Available through www.oed.com.

Palmer, F.R. [1965] 1974. *The English Verb*. 2nd edn. London: Longman.

Poutsma, H. 1904. *A Grammar of Later Modern English*. Part 1, *The Sentence*. 2nd edn. 1929. Groningen: P. Noordhoff.

Poutsma, H. 1926. *A Grammar of Late Modern English*. Part 2, *The Parts of Speech*. Section 2, *The Verb and the Particles*. Groningen: P. Noordhoff.

Poutsma, H. MS. *Dictionary of Constructions of Verbs, Adjectives, and Nouns*. Unpublished. Copyright Oxford University Press.

Radford, Andrew. 1997. *Syntactic Theory and the Structure of English*. Cambridge: Cambridge University Press.

Rohdenburg, G. 2006. The Role of Functional Constraints in the Evolution of the English Complementation System. In *Syntax, Style and Grammatical Norms: English from 1500–2000*, eds. C. Dalton-Puffer, D. Kastovsky, N. Ritt, and H. Schendl, 143–166. Bern: Peter Lang.

Rosenbaum, Peter. 1967. *The Grammar of English Predicate Complement Constructions*. Cambridge, MA: The MIT Press.

Ross, John Robert. 2004. Nouniness. In *Fuzzy Grammar*, eds. Bas Aarts, David Denison, Evelien Keizer, and Gergana Popova, 351–422. Oxford: Oxford University Press.

Rudanko, Juhani. 1996. *Prepositions and Complement Clauses: A Syntactic and Semantic Study of Verbs Governing Prepositions and Complement Clauses in Present-Day English*. Albany, NY: SUNY Press.

Rudanko, Juhani. 2000. *Corpora and Complementation*. Lanham, MD: University Press of America.

Rudanko, Juhani. 2005. Lexico-Grammatical Innovation in Current British and American English: A Case Study on the Transitive *into -ing* Pattern with Evidence from the Bank of English Corpus. *Studia Neophilologica* 77: 171–187.

Rudanko, Juhani. 2006. Watching English Grammar Change. *English Language and Linguistics* 10: 31–48.

Rudanko, Juhani. 2010a. Explaining Grammatical Variation and Change: A Case Study of Complementation in American English over Three Decades. *Journal of English Linguistics* 38: 4–24.

Rudanko, Juhani. 2010b. Change and Variation in Complement Selection: A Case Study from Recent English, with Evidence from Large Corpora. In *Corpus-Linguistic Applications: Current Studies, New Directions*, eds. S. Gries, S. Wulff, and M. Davies, 47–66. Amsterdam: Rodopi.

Rudanko, Juhani. 2011. *Changes in Complementation in British and American English*. Houndmills, Basingstoke: Palgrave Macmillan.

Rudanko, Juhani. 2012. Exploring Aspects of the Great Complement Shift, with Evidence from the *TIME* Corpus and COCA. In *The Oxford Handbook of the History of English*, eds. Terttu Nevalainen and Elizabeth Traugott, 222–232. Oxford: Oxford University Press.

Rudanko, Juhani. 2014. A New Angle on Infinitival and *of -ing* Complements of *Afraid*, with Evidence from the *TIME* Corpus. In *Corpus Interrogation and Grammatical Patterns*, eds. Kristin Davidse, Caroline Gentens, Lobke Ghesquière, and Lieven Vandelanotte, 223–238. Amsterdam: John Benjamins.

Rudanko, Juhani. 2015a. *Linking Form and Meaning: Studies on Selected Control Patterns in Recent English*. Basingstoke: Palgrave Macmillan.

Rudanko, Juhani. 2015b. 'Wheedled Me into Lending Him My Best Hunter': Comparing the Emergence of the Transitive *into -ing* Construction in British and American English. In *Perspectives on Complementation: Structure, Variation and Boundaries*, eds. M. Höglund, P. Rickman, J. Rudanko, and J. Havu. Basingstoke: Palgrave Macmillan.

Sag, Ivan and Carl Pollard. 1991. An Integrated Theory of Complement Control. *Language* 67: 63–113.

Shorter OED = *The New Shorter Oxford English Dictionary on Historical Principles*. 1993. Edited by Lesley Brown. Oxford: Clarendon Press.

Smith, Michael. 2009. The Semantics of Complementation in English: A Cognitive Semantic Account of Two English Complement Constructions. *Language Sciences* 31: 360–388.

Smith, Michael and Joyce Escobedo. 2001. The Semantics of *To*-Infinitival vs. *-Ing* Complement Constructions in English. In *Chicago Linguistic Society CLS 37*. The Main Session, eds. Mary Andronis et al., 549–563. Chicago: Chicago Linguistic Society.

Taylor, John. 2003. Meaning and Context. In *Motivation in Language. Studies in Honour of Günter Radden*, eds. H. Cuyckens, T. Berg, R. Dirven, and K. Panther, 27–48. Amsterdam: John Benjamins.

Vosberg, Uwe. 2003a. The Role of Extractions and *Horror Aequi* in the Evolution of *-ing* Complements in Modern English. In *Determinants of Grammatical Variation in English*, eds. G. Rohdenburg and B. Mondorf, 305–327. Berlin: Mouton de Gruyter.

Vosberg, Uwe. 2003b. Cognitive Complexity and the Establishment of *-ing* Constructions with Retrospective Verbs in Modern English. In *Insights into Late Modern English*, eds. M. Dossena and C. Jones, 197–220. Bern: Peter Lang.

Vosberg, Uwe. 2006. *Die Grosse Komplementverschiebung*. Tübingen: Narr.

Warner, Anthony. 1993. *English Auxiliaries: Structure and History*. Cambridge: Cambridge University Press.

Wulff, Stephanie, Anatol Stefanowitsch, and Stefan T. Gries. 2007. Brutal Brits and Persuasive Americans. In *Aspects of Meaning Construction*, eds. G. Radden, T. Berg, P. Siemund, and K. Köpcke, 265–281. Amsterdam: John Benjamins.

Index

A
Allerton, David, 24, 52

B
Ball, C. N., 13
Berman, Arlene, 18
Bolinger's Principle (Bolinger's Generalization), 2–3, 6, 43, 54, 81
Brezina, Vaclav, 26
Bridgeman, Lorraine, 61–62, 64, 69, 81

C
Chi Square test, 21–22, 32, 49
Choice Principle, 6–7, 16–17, 20–21, 23, 25, 29, 32, 34, 39, 43, 44–55
Chomsky, Noam, 3–5, 42
Collins Cobuild Advanced Learner's Dictionary, 12, 28–29
Control, 7, 25, 42, 51, 58, 59, 80
  object, 7, 58, 59, 70, 74
  subject, 7, 58
Corpus of American Soap Operas, 7–8, 57, 62, 81
Corpus of Contemporary American English, COCA, 7, 44, 47–53, 80
Corpus of Historical American English, COHA, 29–33, 44, 60, 79–80
Corpus of Late Modern English Texts, CLMET, 26n3, 60
CTP, Complement selecting predicate, 2

D
Davies, Mark, 8, 60, 62, 82
Davies, William, 4
Denison, David, 35–36, 40, 79
De Smet, Hendrik, 15
Dowty, David, 19
Dubinsky, Stanley, 3–4
Duffley, Patrick, 20–21, 55n2

E
Escobedo, Joyce, 17–18, 51
Extraction Principle, 16–17, 25, 45, 48, 78, 82

F
Fanego, Teresa, 15–16, 51
Francis, Gill, 61–62, 64, 69, 81

G

Global Web-Based English Corpus, GloWbE, 4, 14–15, 21–23, 36–39, 62–63, 69
Goldberg, Adele, 60, 66
Great Complement Shift, 15–16, 23, 29, 32, 34, 79, 82

H

Herbst, Thomas, 12
Höglund, Mikko, 55n1
Huddleston, Rodney, 1–2, 33, 45
Hundt, Marianne, 18
Hunston, Susan, 61

J

Jackendoff, Ray, 18
Jespersen, Otto, 3

K

Kuno, Susumu, 18

L

Leech, Geoffrey, 8

M

Mair, Christian, 20–21
Meyerhoff, Miriam, 26n2
Mukherjee, Joybrato, 26n2

N

Non-agentive reinterpretation, 34, 38
Noonan, Michael, 2

O

Oxford Advanced Learner's Dictionary, 12, 28, 42
Oxford English Dictionary, OED, 11–12, 43, 51, 53, 61, 67, 69–70, 73

P

Palmer, Frank, 19
Pollard, Carl, 70
Poutsma, H., 9n1, 12, 15, 25, 26n3, 28
Pullum, Geoffrey, 1–2, 45

R

Radford, Andrew, 5
Rohdenburg, Günter, 15, 16, 34
Rosenbaum, Peter, 3, 9n1
Ross, John Robert, 40n1
Rudanko, Juhani, 13, 16, 18, 19, 20, 24, 25, 44, 52, 54, 59, 60, 62, 68, 69, 74, 81

S

Sag, Ivan, 70
Shorter OED, 65–66, 68, 72–73
Smith, Michael, 17–18, 51

T

Taylor, Robert, 19

V

Vosberg, Uwe, 16, 53
VP Deletion, 5, 9n2, 35–36, 40, 79

W

Warner, Anthony, 9n2, 35, 79
Wulff, Stephanie, 73